TensorFlow 2.0

Use the new and improved features of TensorFlow to
enhance machine learning and deep learning

Ajay Baranwal
Alizishaan Khatri
Tanish Baranwal

BIRMINGHAM - MUMBAI

What's New in TensorFlow 2.0

Commissioning Editor: Mrinmayee Kawalkar
Acquisition Editor: Snehal Main
Content Development Editor: Athikho Sapuni Rishana
Senior Editor: Sophie Rogers
Technical Editor: Joseph Sunil
Copy Editor: Safis Editing
Project Coordinator: Kirti Pisat
Proofreader: Safis Editing
Indexer: Priyanka Dhadke
Production Designer: Jyoti Chauhan

First published: August 2019

Production reference: 1080819

Published by Packt Publishing Ltd.
Livery Place
35 Livery Street
Birmingham
B3 2PB, UK.

ISBN 978-1-83882-385-6

www.packtpub.com

Contributors

About the authors

Ajay Baranwal works as a director at the Center for Deep Learning in Electronics Manufacturing, where he is responsible for researching and developing TensorFlow-based deep learning applications in the semiconductor and electronics manufacturing industry. Part of his role is to teach and train deep learning techniques to professionals.

He has a solid history of software engineering and management, where he got hooked on deep learning. He moved to **natural language understanding** (NLU) to pursue deep learning further at Abzooba and built an information retrieval system for the finance sector. He has also worked at Ansys Inc. as a senior manager (engineering) and a technical fellow (data science) and introduced several ML applications.

Alizishaan Khatri works as a machine learning engineer in Silicon Valley. He uses TensorFlow to build, design, and maintain production-grade systems that use deep learning for NLP applications. A major system he has built is a deep learning-based system for detecting offensive content in chats. Other works he has done includes text classification and **named entity recognition** (NER) systems for different use cases. He is passionate about sharing ideas with the community and frequently speaks at tech conferences across the globe.

He holds a master's degree in computer science from the SUNY Buffalo University. His thesis proposed a solution to the problem of overfitting in deep learning. Outside of his work, he enjoys skiing and mountaineering.

Tanish Baranwal is a sophomore in high school and lives in California with his family and has worked with his dad on deep learning projects using TensorFlow for the last 3 years. He has been coding for 9 years (since 1st grade) and is well versed in Python and JavaScript. He is now learning C++. He has certificates from various online courses and has won the Entrepreneurship Showcase Award at his school.

Some of his deep learning projects include anomaly detection systems for transaction fraud, a system to save energy by turning off domestic water heaters when not in use, and a fully functional style transfer program that can recreate any photograph in another style. He has also written blogs on deep learning on Medium with over 1,000 views.

About the reviewers

Jay Kim is an experienced data scientist who has broad experience in data science, AI, machine learning, deep learning, and statistical analysis. He has broad experience in various industries, such as utilities, the automotive sector, manufacturing, commercial, and research.

Narotam Singh has been actively involved in various technical programs and the training of **Government of India** (**GoI**) officers in the fields of information technology and communication. He did his master's degree in the field of electronics, and graduated with honors in physics. He also holds a diploma in computer engineering and a postgraduate diploma in computer applications. Presently, he works as a freelancer. He has many research publications to his name and is also a technical reviewer of various books. His present research interests involve artificial intelligence, machine learning, deep learning, robotics, and spirituality.

Packt is searching for authors like you

If you're interested in becoming an author for Packt, please visit `authors.packtpub.com` and apply today. We have worked with thousands of developers and tech professionals, just like you, to help them share their insight with the global tech community. You can make a general application, apply for a specific hot topic that we are recruiting an author for, or submit your own idea.

Packt>

Table of Contents

Section 2: TensorFlow 2.0 - Data and Model Training Pipelines

Section 3: TensorFlow 2.0 - Model Inference and Deployment and AIY

Preface

TensorFlow is one of the most popular machine learning frameworks, and its new version, TensorFlow 2.0, improves its simplicity and ease of use. This book will help you understand and utilize the latest TensorFlow features.

What's New in TensorFlow 2.0 starts by focusing on advanced concepts such as the new TensorFlow Keras APIs, eager execution, and efficient distribution strategies that help you to run your machine learning models on multiple GPUs and TPUs. The book then takes you through the process of building data ingestion and training pipelines, and it provides recommendations and best practices for feeding data to models created using the new `tf.keras` API. You'll explore the process of building an inference pipeline using TensorFlow Serving and other multi-platform deployments before moving on to explore the newly released AIY which is essentially do-it-yourself AI. This book delves into the core APIs to help you build unified convolutional and recurrent layers and use TensorBoard to visualize deep learning models using what-if analysis.

By the end of the book, you'll have learned about the compatibility between TensorFlow 2.0 and TensorFlow 1.x and will be able to smoothly migrate to TensorFlow 2.0.

Who this book is for

If you're a data scientist, machine learning practitioner, deep learning researcher, or AI enthusiast who wants to migrate code to, and explore the latest features of TensorFlow 2.0, this book is for you. Prior experience with TensorFlow and Python programming is necessary to understand the concepts covered in the book.

What this book covers

Chapter 1, *Getting Started with TensorFlow 2.0*, provides a quick bird's-eye view of the architectural and API-level changes in TensorFlow 2.0. It covers TensorFlow 2.0 installation and setup, compares how it has changed compared to TensorFlow 1.x (such as Keras APIs and layer APIs), and also presents the addition of rich extensions such as TensorFlow Probability, Tensor2Tensor, Ragged Tensors, and the newly available custom training logic for loss functions.

Chapter 2, *Keras Default Integration and Eager Execution*, goes deeper into high-level TensorFlow 2.0 APIs using Keras. It presents a detailed perspective of how graphs are evaluated in TensorFlow 1.x compared to TensorFlow 2.0. It explains lazy evaluation and eager execution and how they are different in TensorFlow 2.0, and it also shows how to use Keras model subclassing to incorporate TensorFlow 2.0 lower APIs for custom-built models.

Chapter 3, *Designing and Constructing Input Data Pipelines*, gives an overview of how to build complex input data pipelines for ingesting large training and inference datasets in most common formats, such as CSV, images, and text using TFRecords and tf.data.Dataset. It gives a general explanation of protocol buffers and protocol messages and how are they implemented using tf.Example. It also explains the best practices of using tf.data.Dataset with regard to the shuffling, prefetching, and batching of data, and provides recommendations for building data pipelines.

Chapter 4, *Model Training and Use of TensorBoard*, covers an overall model training pipeline to enable you to build, train, and validate state-of-the-art models. It talks about how to integrate input data pipelines, create tf.keras models, run training in a distributed manner, and run validations to fine-tune hyperparameters. It explains how to export TensorFlow models for deployment or inferencing, and it outlines the usage of TensorBoard, the changes to it in TensorFlow 2.0, and how to use it for debugging and profiling a model's speed and performance.

Chapter 5, *Model Inference Pipelines – Multi-platform Deployments*, shows us some deployment strategies for using the trained model to build software applications at scale in a live production environment. Models trained in TensorFlow 2.0 can be deployed on platforms such as servers and web browsers using a variety of programming languages, such as Python and JavaScript.

Chapter 6, *AIY Projects and TensorFlow Lite*, shows us how to deploy models trained in TensorFlow 2.0 on low-powered embedded systems such as edge devices and mobile systems including Android, iOS, the Raspberry Pi, Edge TPUs, and the NVIDIA Jetson Nano. It also contains details about training and deploying models on Google's AIY kits.

Chapter 7, *Migrating From TensorFlow 1.x to 2.0*, shows us the conceptual differences between TensorFlow 1.x and TensorFlow 2.0, the compatibility criteria between them, and ways to migrate between them, syntactically and semantically. It also shows several examples of syntactic and semantic migration from TensorFlow 1.x to TensorFlow 2.0, and contains references and future information.

To get the most out of this book

The reader needs to have basic knowledge of Python and TensorFlow.

Download the example code files

You can download the example code files for this book from your account at `www.packt.com`. If you purchased this book elsewhere, you can visit `www.packt.com/support` and register to have the files emailed directly to you.

You can download the code files by following these steps:

1. Log in or register at `www.packt.com`.
2. Select the **SUPPORT** tab.
3. Click on **Code Downloads & Errata**.
4. Enter the name of the book in the **Search** box and follow the onscreen instructions.

Once the file is downloaded, please make sure that you unzip or extract the folder using the latest version of:

- WinRAR/7-Zip for Windows
- Zipeg/iZip/UnRarX for Mac
- 7-Zip/PeaZip for Linux

The code bundle for the book is also hosted on GitHub at `https://github.com/PacktPublishing/What-s-New-in-TensorFlow-2.0`. In case there's an update to the code, it will be updated on the existing GitHub repository.

We also have other code bundles from our rich catalog of books and videos available at `https://github.com/PacktPublishing/`. Check them out!

Download the color images

We also provide a PDF file that has color images of the screenshots/diagrams used in this book. You can download it here: `http://www.packtpub.com/sites/default/files/downloads/9781838823856_ColorImages.pdf`.

Conventions used

There are a number of text conventions used throughout this book.

`CodeInText`: Indicates code words in text, database table names, folder names, filenames, file extensions, pathnames, dummy URLs, user input, and Twitter handles. Here is an example: "Mount the downloaded `WebStorm-10*.dmg` disk image file as another disk in your system."

A block of code is set as follows:

```
layer_name = tf.keras.Input(
    shape=None,
    batch_size=None,
    name=None,
    dtype=None,
    sparse=False,
    tensor=None,
    **kwargs
)
```

Any command-line input or output is written as follows:

```
python3 -m pip --help
```

Bold: Indicates a new term, an important word, or words that you see onscreen. For example, words in menus or dialog boxes appear in the text like this. Here is an example: "**Eager execution** is an imperative programming environment that evaluates operations immediately, without building graphs."

Warnings or important notes appear like this.

Tips and tricks appear like this.

Get in touch

Feedback from our readers is always welcome.

General feedback: If you have questions about any aspect of this book, mention the book title in the subject of your message and email us at customercare@packtpub.com.

Errata: Although we have taken every care to ensure the accuracy of our content, mistakes do happen. If you have found a mistake in this book, we would be grateful if you would report this to us. Please visit www.packt.com/submit-errata, selecting your book, clicking on the Errata Submission Form link, and entering the details.

Piracy: If you come across any illegal copies of our works in any form on the Internet, we would be grateful if you would provide us with the location address or website name. Please contact us at copyright@packt.com with a link to the material.

If you are interested in becoming an author: If there is a topic that you have expertise in and you are interested in either writing or contributing to a book, please visit authors.packtpub.com.

Reviews

Please leave a review. Once you have read and used this book, why not leave a review on the site that you purchased it from? Potential readers can then see and use your unbiased opinion to make purchase decisions, we at Packt can understand what you think about our products, and our authors can see your feedback on their book. Thank you!

For more information about Packt, please visit packt.com.

Section 1: TensorFlow 2.0 - Architecture and API Changes

1

This section of the book will give you a quick summary of what is new in TensorFlow 2.0, a comparison with TensorFlow 1.x, the differences between lazy evaluation and eager execution, changes at the architectural level, and API usage with respect to `tf.keras` and `Estimator`.

This section contains the following chapters:

- Chapter 1, *Getting Started with TensorFlow 2.0*
- Chapter 2, *Keras Default Integration and Eager Execution*

1
Getting Started with TensorFlow 2.0

This book aims to familiarize readers with the new features introduced in **TensorFlow 2.0** (**TF 2.0**) and to empower you to unlock its potential while building machine learning applications. This chapter provides a bird's-eye view of new architectural and API-level changes in TF 2.0. We will cover TF 2.0 installation and setup, and will compare the changes with respect to **TensorFlow 1.x** (**TF 1.x**), such as Keras APIs and layer APIs. We will also cover the addition of rich extensions, such as TensorFlow Probability, Tensor2Tensor, Ragged Tensors, and the newly available custom training logic for loss functions. This chapter also summarizes the changes to the layers API and other APIs.

The following topics will be covered in this chapter:

- What's new?
- TF 2.0 installation and setup
- Using TF 2.0
- Rich extensions

Technical requirements

You will need the following before you can start executing the steps described in the sections ahead:

- Python 3.4 or higher
- A computer with Ubuntu 16.04 or later (The instructions remain similar for most *NIX-based systems such as macOS or other Linux variants)

What's new?

The philosophy of TF 2.0 is based on simplicity and ease of use. The major updates include easy model building with `tf.keras` and eager execution, robust model deployment for production and commercial use for any platform, powerful experimentation techniques and tools for research, and API simplification for a more intuitive organization of APIs.

The new organization of TF 2.0 is simplified by the following diagram:

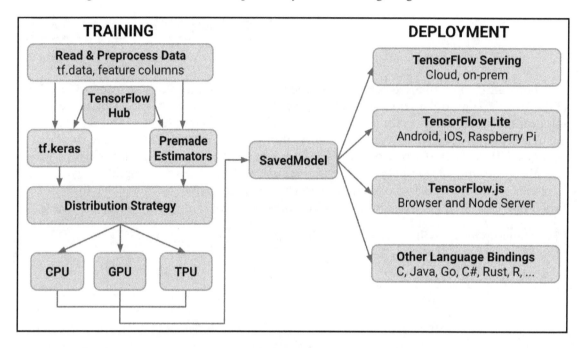

The preceding diagram is focused on using the Python API for training and deploying; however, the same process is followed with the other supported languages including Julia, JavaScript, and R. The flow of TF 2.0 is separated into two sections—model training and model deployment, where model training includes the data pipelines, model creation, training, and distribution strategies; and model deployment includes the variety of means of deployment, such as TF Serving, TFLite, TF.js, and other language bindings. The components in this diagram will each be elaborated upon in their respective chapters.

The biggest change in TF 2.0 is the addition of eager execution. **Eager execution** is an imperative programming environment that evaluates operations immediately, without necessarily building graphs. All operations return concrete values instead of constructing a computational graph that the user can compute later.

This makes it significantly easier to build and train TensorFlow models and reduces much of the boilerplate code that was attributed to TF 1.x code. Eager execution has an intuitive interface that follows the standard Python code flow. Code written in eager execution is also much easier to debug, as standard Python modules for debugging, such as `pdb`, can be used to inspect code for sources of error. The creation of custom models is also easier due to the natural Python control flow and support for iteration.

Another major change in TF 2.0 is the migration to `tf.keras` as the standard module for creating and training TensorFlow models. The Keras API is the central high-level API in TF 2.0, making it easy to get started with TensorFlow. Although Keras is an independent implementation of deep learning concepts, the `tf.keras` implementation contains enhancements such as eager execution for immediate iteration and debugging, and `tf.data` is also included for building scalable input pipelines.

An example workflow in `tf.keras` would be to first load the data using the `tf.data` module. This allows for large amounts of data to be streamed from the disk without storing all of the data in memory. Then, the developer builds, trains, and validates the model using `tf.keras` or the premade estimators. The next step would be to run the model and debug it using the benefits of eager execution. Once the model is ready for full-fledged training, use a distribution strategy for distributed training. Finally, when the model is ready for deployment, export the model to a `SavedModel` module for deployment through any of the distribution strategies shown in the diagram.

Changes from TF 1.x

The first major difference between TF 1.x and TF 2.0 is the API organization. TF 2.0 has reduced the redundancies in the API structure. Major changes include the removal of `tf.app`, `tf.flags`, and `tf.logging` in favor of other Python modules, such as `absl-py` and the built-in logging function.

The `tf.contrib` library is also now removed from the main TensorFlow repo. The code implemented in this library has either been moved to a different location or has been shifted to the TensorFlow add-ons library. The reason for this move is that the `contrib` module had grown beyond what could be maintained in a single repository.

Other changes include the removal of the `QueueRunner` module in favor of using `tf.data`, the removal of graph collections, and changes in how variables are treated. The `QueueRunner` module was a way of providing data to a model for training, but was quite complicated and harder to use than `tf.data`, which is now the default way of feeding data to a model. Other benefits of using `tf.data` for the data pipeline are explained in Chapter 3, *Designing and Constructing Input Data Pipelines*.

Another major change in TF 2.0 is that there are no more global variables. In TF 1.x, variables created using `tf.Variable` would be put on the default graph and would still be recoverable through their names. TF 1.x had all sorts of mechanisms as an attempt to help users to recover their variables, such as variable scopes, global collections, and helper methods such as `tf.get_global_step` and `tf.global_variables_initializer`. All of this is removed in TF 2.0 for the default variable behavior in Python.

TF 2.0 installation and setup

This section describes the steps required to install TF 2.0 on your system using different methods and on different system configurations. Entry-level users are recommended to start with the `pip`- and `virtualenv`-based methods. For users of the GPU version, `docker` is the recommended method.

Installing and using pip

For the uninitiated, `pip` is a popular package management system in the Python community. If this is not installed on your system, please install it before proceeding further. On many Linux installations, Python and `pip` are installed by default. You can check whether `pip` is installed by typing the following command:

```
python3 -m pip --help
```

If you see a `blurb` describing the different commands that `pip` supports, `pip` is installed on your system. If `pip` is not installed, you will see an error message, which will be something similar to `No module named pip`.

It usually is a good idea to isolate your development environment. This greatly simplifies dependency management and streamlines the software development process. We can achieve environment isolation by using a tool in Python called `virtualenv`. This step is optional but highly recommended:

```
>>mkdir .venv
>>virtualenv --python=python3.6 .venv/
>>source .venv.bin/activate
```

You can install TensorFlow using `pip`, as shown in the following command:

```
pip3 install tensorflow==version_tag
```

For example, if you want to install version `2.0.0-beta1`, your command should be as follows:

```
pip3 install tensorflow==2.0.0-beta1
```

 A complete list of the most recent package updates is available at `https:/ /pypi.org/project/tensorflow/#history`.

You can test your installation by running the following command:

```
python3 -c "import tensorflow as tf; a = tf.constant(1);
print(tf.math.add(a, a))"
```

Using Docker

If you would like to isolate your TensorFlow installation from the rest of your system, you might want to consider installing it using a Docker image. This would require you to have Docker installed on your system. Installation instructions are available at `https://docs.docker.com/install/`.

 In order to use Docker without `sudo` on a Linux system, please follow the post-install steps at:
`https://docs.docker.com/install/linux/linux-postinstall/`.

The TensorFlow team officially supports Docker images as a mode of installation. To the user, one implication of this is that updated Docker images will be made available for download at `https://hub.docker.com/r/tensorflow/tensorflow/`.

Download a Docker image locally using the following command:

```
docker pull tensorflow/tensorflow:YOUR_TAG_HERE
```

The previous command should've downloaded the Docker image from the centralized repository. To run the code using this image, you need to start a new container and type the following:

```
docker run -it --rm tensorflow/tensorflow:YOUR_TAG_HERE \
    python -c "import tensorflow as tf; a = tf.constant(1);
print(tf.math.add(a, a))"
```

A Docker-based installation is also a good option if you intend to use GPUs. Detailed instructions for this are provided in the next section.

GPU installation

Installing the GPU version of TensorFlow is slightly different from the process for the CPU version. It can be installed using both `pip` and Docker. The choice of installation process boils down to the end objective. The Docker-based process is easier as it involves installing fewer additional components. It also helps avoid library conflict. This can, though, introduce an additional overhead of managing the container environment. The `pip`-based version involves installing more additional components but offers a greater degree of flexibility and efficiency. It enables the resultant installation to run directly on the local host without any virtualization.

To proceed, assuming you have the necessary hardware set up, you would need the following piece of software at a minimum. Detailed instructions for installation are provided in the link for NVIDIA GPU drivers (`https://www.nvidia.com/Download/index.aspx?lang=en-us`).

Installing using Docker

At the time of writing this book, this option is only available for NVIDIA GPUs running on Linux hosts. If you meet the platform constraints, then this is an excellent option as it significantly simplifies the process. It also minimizes the number of additional software components that you need to install by leveraging a pre-built container. To proceed, we need to install `nvidia-docker`. Please refer the following links for additional details:

- Installation: `https://github.com/NVIDIA/nvidia-docker`
- FAQs: `https://github.com/NVIDIA/nvidia-docker/wiki/Frequently-Asked-Questions#platform-support`

Once you've completed the steps described in the preceding links, take the following steps:

1. Test whether the GPU is available:

   ```
   lspci | grep -i nvidia
   ```

2. Verify your `nvidia-docker` installation (for `v2` of `nvidia-docker`):

   ```
   docker run --runtime=nvidia --rm nvidia/cuda nvidia-smi
   ```

3. Download a Docker image locally:

   ```
   docker pull tensorflow/tensorflow:YOUR_TAG_HERE
   ```

4. Let's say you're trying to run the most recent version of the GPU-based image. You'd type the following:

   ```
   docker pull tensorflow/tensorflow:latest-gpu
   ```

5. Start the container and run the code:

   ```
   docker run --runtime=nvidia -it --rm tensorflow/tensorflow:latest-gpu \
        python -c "import tensorflow as tf; a = tf.constant(1);
   print(tf.math.add(a, a))"
   ```

Installing using pip

If you would like to use TensorFlow with an NVIDIA GPU, you need to install the following additional pieces of software on your system. Detailed instructions for installation are provided in the links shared:

- CUDA Toolkit: TensorFlow supports CUDA 10.0 (https://developer.nvidia.com/cuda-toolkit-archive)
- CUPTI ships with the CUDA Toolkit (https://docs.nvidia.com/cuda/cupti/)
- The cuDNN SDK (version 7.4.1 or above) (https://developer.nvidia.com/cudnn)
- (Optional) TensorRT 5.0 to improve latency and throughput for inference on some models (https://docs.nvidia.com/deeplearning/sdk/tensorrt-install-guide/index.html)

Once all the previous components have been installed, this is a fairly straightforward process.

Install TensorFlow using `pip`:

```
pip3 install tensorflow-gpu==version_tag
```

For example, if you want to install `tensorflow-2.0:alpha`, then you'd have to type in the following command:

```
pip3 install tensorflow-gpu==2.0.0-alpha0
```

A complete list of the most recent package updates is available at `https://pypi.org/project/tensorflow/#history`.

You can test your installation by running the following command:

```
python3 -c "import tensorflow as tf; a = tf.constant(1);
print(tf.math.add(a, a))"
```

Using TF 2.0

TF 2.0 can be used in two main ways—using low-level APIs and using high-level APIs. To use the low-level APIs in TF 2.0, APIs such as `tf.GradientTape` and `tf.function` are implemented.

The code flow for writing low-level code is to define a forward pass inside of a function that takes the input data as an argument. This function is then annotated with the `tf.function` decorator in order to run it in graph mode along with all of its benefits. To record and get the gradients of the forward pass, both the decorator function and the loss function are run inside the `tf.GradientTape` context manager, from which gradients can be calculated and applied on the model variables.

Training code can also be written using the low-level APIs for `tf.keras` models by using `tf.GradientTape`. This is for when more control and customizability is needed over the default `tf.keras.Model.fit` method. Training methods and pipelines are explained in depth in Chapter 4, *Model Training and Use of TensorBoard*.

The simple comparison between TF 2.0 and TF 1.x is that the tensor that is run using `sess.run` in TF 1.x is now a function, and the feed dict and placeholders are the arguments of that function. This is the philosophical change between TF 2.0 and TF 1.x; there is a shift toward complete object-oriented code where all APIs and modules are callable objects.

Using the high-level APIs in TF 2.0 is easier, where `tf.keras` is the default high-level API used. `tf.keras` has three different methods of model creation. These methods are as follows:

- **The Sequential API**: This is another change brought on in TF 2.0. The previous high-level API for model creation in TF 1.x was the `tf.layers` module. This module has been converted to `tf.keras.layers`, where nearly all the methods from the `tf.layers` module are replicated in `tf.keras.layers`. This makes it easy to convert from `tf.layers` to `tf.keras.layers`, as the code is nearly completely identical.

  Using the `Sequential` API to create a model is done by creating a linear model with the symbolic `tf.keras` layer classes. This style is used for completely linear models and is the easiest style to use.

  The following code block is an example of a `Sequential` API model:

  ```
  model = tf.keras.Sequential([
      tf.keras.layers.Conv2D(32, 3, activation='relu',
  kernel_regularizer=tf.keras.regularizers.l2(0.04),
                          input_shape=(28, 28, 1)),
      tf.keras.layers.MaxPooling2D(),
      tf.keras.layers.Flatten(),
      tf.keras.layers.Dropout(0.1),
      tf.keras.layers.Dense(64, activation='relu'),
      tf.keras.layers.BatchNormalization(),
      tf.keras.layers.Dense(10, activation='softmax')
  ])

  train_data = tf.ones(shape=(1, 28, 28, 1))
  test_data = tf.ones(shape=(1, 28, 28, 1))

  train_out = model(train_data, training=True)

  test_out = model(test_data, training=False)
  ```

- **The functional API**: This API has more flexibility than the `Sequential` API in the sense that it's based on calling the layer classes on the output tensor of the layer preceding it. This means that non-linear models and architectures can be implemented, such as the Inception and ResNet architectures.

The following code block is an example of a model created with the `functional` API:

```python
encoder_input = keras.Input(shape=(28, 28, 1), name='img')
x = layers.Conv2D(16, 3, activation='relu')(encoder_input)
x = layers.Conv2D(32, 3, activation='relu')(x)
x = layers.MaxPooling2D(3)(x)
x = layers.Conv2D(32, 3, activation='relu')(x)
x = layers.Conv2D(16, 3, activation='relu')(x)
encoder_output = layers.GlobalMaxPooling2D()(x)

encoder = keras.Model(encoder_input, encoder_output,
name='encoder')
```

- **The model subclassing technique**: This is very similar to the low-level approach in the sense that it is used to create custom models and layers that implement technologies and techniques not included in TensorFlow. The model subclassing technique involves creating a class that inherits from the `tf.keras.Model` base class and has a call method defined that takes an input argument and a training argument, and then computes and returns the result of a forward pass through the model.

The following code block is an example of a model created with model subclassing:

```python
class ResNet(tf.keras.Model):

    def __init__(self):
        super(ResNet, self).__init__()
        self.block_1 = ResNetBlock()
        self.block_2 = ResNetBlock()
        self.global_pool = layers.GlobalAveragePooling2D()
        self.classifier = Dense(num_classes)

    def call(self, inputs):
        x = self.block_1(inputs)
        x = self.block_2(x)
        x = self.global_pool(x)
        return self.classifier(x)

resnet = ResNet()
dataset = ...
resnet.fit(dataset, epochs=10)
```

Rich extensions

Rich extensions are a set of features that have been introduced in TensorFlow to boost user productivity and expand capabilities. In this section, we will cover Ragged Tensors and how to use them, and, we will also cover the new modules introduced in TF 2.0.

Ragged Tensors

Variable-sized data is a common occurrence when both training and serving machine learning models. This issue is constant across the different underlying media types and model architectures. The contemporary solution is to use the size of the largest record, and use padding for smaller records. This is inefficient, not only in terms of memory or storage, but also computational efficiency; for example, when dealing with inputs to a recurrent model.

Ragged Tensors help address this issue. At a very high level, Ragged Tensors can be thought of as the TensorFlow analogs of variable-length linked lists. An important fact to note here is that this variability can be present in nested dimensions as well. This means that it is possible to have a list of variable-sized elements. Generalizing this property to multiple dimensions opens doors to a variety of interesting use cases. One of the important restrictions to keep in mind, though, is that all values in a Ragged Tensor must be of the same type. Some commonly non-uniform shaped data types that Ragged Tensors can be used for includes the following:

- Variable-length features:
  - Example—the number of characters in a word
- Batches of variable-length sequential inputs:
  - Example—sentences, time-series data, and audio clips
- Hierarchical inputs:
  - Example—text documents that are subdivided into sections, paragraphs, sentences, words and characters; organizational hierarchies
- Individual fields in structured inputs:
  - Example—HTTP Request payloads, protocol buffers, and JSON data

In the following subsections, we shall look at the main properties of Ragged Tensors and write some code to see them in action.

What are Ragged Tensors, really?

Ragged Tensors can also be defined as tensors with one or more ragged dimensions; in other words, dimensions with variable-length slices. As most common use-cases involve dealing with a finite number of records, Ragged Tensors require the outermost dimension to be uniform, in other words, that all slices of that dimension should have the same length. Dimensions preceding the outermost dimension can be both ragged and uniform. To summarize these points, we can state that the shape of a Ragged Tensor is currently restricted to the following form:

- A single uniform dimension
- Followed by one or more ragged dimensions
- Followed by zero or more uniform dimensions

Constructing a Ragged Tensor

TF 2.0 provides a large number of methods that can be used to create or return Ragged Tensors. One of the most straightforward ones is `tf.ragged.constant()`. Let's use it to create a Ragged Tensor of dimension (num_sentences, (num_words)). Please note that we've used round brackets to indicate the dimension that is ragged:

```
sentences = tf.ragged.constant([
                    ["Hello", "World", "!"],
                    ["We", "are", "testing", "tf.ragged.constant", "."]
           ])
print(sentences)
```

You should see something like this:

```
<tf.RaggedTensor [[b'Hello', b'World', b'!'], [b'We', b'are', b'testing',
b'tf.ragged.constant', b'.']]>
```

It is also possible to create a Ragged Tensor from an old-style tensor or Python list with padded elements. This can be very useful in building efficient TF 2.0 models that consume data from a lower-stage pipeline written for earlier versions of TensorFlow. The functionality is exposed by the `tf.RaggedTensor.from_tensor()` function. The padding value is provided by the `padding` keyword argument. If used correctly, this can provide users with significant amounts of memory, especially in cases of sparse arrays.

Consider the following example in which we define a Python list. Each element of this list has a further list containing a variable number of numerical values. Some of the numbers listed here are padded values and are indicated by the digit 0. This can also be looked at as a matrix of 4 records containing 5 attributes each; in other words, a 4 x 5 matrix:

```
x = [
        [1, 7, 0, 0, 0],
        [2, 0, 0, 0, 0],
        [4, 5, 8, 9, 1],
        [1, 0, 0, 0, 0]
    ]
print(tf.RaggedTensor.from_tensor(x, padding=0))
```

We can see that a majority of records in the preceding matrix contain padding values. These values occupy memory. As seen in the following output, converting the preceding matrix to a Ragged Tensor eliminates the lagging 0 (padding) values. This results in a memory-efficient representation of the data:

```
<tf.RaggedTensor [[1, 7], [2], [4, 5, 8, 9, 1], [1]]>
```

The preceding example is a small illustration of how using ragged representations saves memory. As the number of records and/or dimensions grow, the memory savings provided by this representation would become more pronounced.

Basic operations on Ragged Tensors

Ragged Tensors can be used in a manner similar to regular tensors in many cases. TensorFlow provides over 100 operators that support Ragged Tensors. These operators can be broadly classified as fundamental mathematical operators, array operators, or string operators, among others.

The following code block shows the process of adding two Ragged Tensors:

```
x = tf.ragged.constant([
                        [1, 2, 3, 4],
                        [1, 2]
                      ])
y = tf.ragged.constant([
                        [4, 3, 2, 1],
                        [5, 6]
                      ])
print(tf.add(x, y))
```

This results in the following output:

```
<tf.RaggedTensor [[5, 5, 5, 5], [6, 8]]>
```

Another interesting feature is that operator overloading is defined for Ragged Tensors. This means that a programmer can intuitively use operators such as +, -, *, /, //, %, **, &, |, ^, <, <=, >, and >=, just like they would with other tensors.

The following code block shows the multiplication of a Ragged Tensor using an overloaded operator:

```
x = tf.ragged.constant([
                        [1, 2, 3, 4],
                        [1, 2]
                       ])
print(x * 2)   # Multiply a ragged tensor with a scalar
print(x * x)   # Multiply a ragged tensor with another ragged tensor
```

The resultant output is as follows:

```
<tf.RaggedTensor [[2, 4, 6, 8], [2, 4]]>
<tf.RaggedTensor [[1, 4, 9, 16], [1, 4]]>
```

In addition, a variety of Ragged Tensor-specific operators are defined in the `tf.ragged` package. It could be worthwhile to check out the documentation of the package to learn more. Please see the following links for detailed documentation on this:

- https://www.tensorflow.org/versions/r2.0/api_docs/python/tf/RaggedTensor
- https://www.tensorflow.org/versions/r2.0/api_docs/python/tf/ragged

New and important packages

The arrival of TF 2.0 also comes with the arrival of many more interesting and useful packages under TensorFlow that can be installed separately. Some of these packages include TensorFlow Datasets, TensorFlow Addons, TensorFlow Text, and TensorFlow Probability.

TensorFlow Datasets is a Python module that provides easy access to over 100 datasets, ranging from audio to natural language to images. These datasets can be easily downloaded and used in models via the following code:

```
import tensorflow_datasets as tfds
dataset = tfds.load(name="mnist", split=tfds.Split.TRAIN)
dataset =
dataset.shuffle(1024).batch(32).prefetch(tf.data.experimental.AUTOTUNE)
```

 Datasets taken from this library are tf.data.Dataset objects, which means that all tf.data methods can be used to modify the base dataset. More details on the TensorFlow datasets module are in Chapter 3, *Designing and Constructing Input Data Pipelines*.

TensorFlow Addons (**TF Addons**) is another TensorFlow module. This module contains most of the tf.contrib module from TF 1.x, other than the methods that were moved into the main tf module. TF Addons contains many experimental and state-of-the-art layers, loss functions, initializers, and optimizers, all in the form of TF 2.0 objects. This means that APIs taken from TF Addons can be seamlessly incorporated into a normal tf.keras model without any extra changes.

TensorFlow Text is a very recent module, which adds NLP APIs to TF 2.0. This module includes methods such as sentence and word tokenization, among other popular techniques in the NLP field. Something to note is that this module is very new and so is subject to multiple changes in the API structure.

TensorFlow Probability is a module that adds APIs for probability calculations in TensorFlow. This module allows researchers and developers to take advantage of TensorFlow's optimized operations and computations in order to perform a multitude of probability-related tasks.

All the aforementioned packages can be installed using pip and by installing in the tensorflow-module format.

Summary

TF 2.0 contains many major changes, such as API cleanup, eager execution, and an object-oriented philosophy. The API cleanup includes deprecating redundant modules that have equivalent standard Python libraries, as well as removing and reorganizing the `tf.contrib` module into the main API and into the TensorFlow Addons package. Eager execution and object-oriented APIs allow debugging to be much more efficient and straightforward, and also lead to variables being treated as normal Python variables. This means that variable collections and other APIs dedicated to dealing with global variables are no longer needed, and thus are removed in TF 2.0.

TF 2.0 also shifts the default high-level API from estimators in TF 1.x to `tf.keras` in TF 2.0 for both simplicity and scalability. The `tf.keras` API has three different programming types, each providing different levels of abstraction and customizability. Low-level TF 2.0 code can be written using `tf.GradientTape` to handle gradients of operations, and `tf.function` for graph-based execution.

This chapter also covered the different ways to install TF 2.0, including installation through `pip` and Docker, as well as the installation of the GPU version. There are many modules that are compatible with and have been released alongside TF 2.0, which further enhance and augment the possibilities of the base API. These include TensorFlow Datasets, TensorFlow Addons, TensorFlow Text, and TensorFlow Probability.

This chapter also included Ragged Tensors, which are useful for storing data with variable length and shape and hierarchical inputs. This means that Ragged Tensors are useful for storing language and sequence data.

In the next chapter, we will learn about Keras' default integration and eager execution.

2
Keras Default Integration and Eager Execution

This chapter covers two high-level **TensorFlow 2.0** (**TF 2.0**) APIs—Keras and Estimators. Focusing on the concepts of lazy evaluation and eager execution, this chapter highlights the difference between how the underlying compute graphs are evaluated in **TensorFlow 1.x** (**TF 1.x**) and TF 2.0. This chapter also presents a detailed guide on building custom models (using custom low-level operations) using a high-level API such as Keras.

The following topics will be covered in this chapter:

- New abstractions in TF 2.0
- Diving deep into the Keras API
- Estimators
- Evaluating TensorFlow graphs

Technical requirements

In order to run the code excerpts given in this chapter, you will need the following hardware and software:

- TF 2.0 or higher (either of the CPU or GPU versions will suffice)
- Python 3.4+ (currently, the highest Python version supported by TensorFlow is 3.6)
- NumPy (if not automatically installed by TensorFlow)

The code files for this chapter are available at `https://github.com/PacktPublishing/What-s-New-in-TensorFlow-2.0/tree/master/Chapter02`.

New abstractions in TF 2.0

Abstractions are a very popular tool used in the process of programming and software development. In a very high-level sense, an **abstraction** refers to the process of isolating and describing the central idea of a particular task or set of tasks without necessarily specifying the physical, spatial, or temporal details. When done right, an abstraction can significantly reduce the amount of code that needs to be written for a particular task. It also boosts the reusability of existing code and makes it compatible with TF 2.0.

While working with machine learning systems, there are some common high-level tasks, such as training data, modeling, model evaluation, prediction, model storing, and model loading, that are common across a wide variety of tasks. An end programmer might also want to just modify one small component of the application while leaving the rest unchanged. Thus, it becomes a good idea to leverage the power of abstraction to optimize user experience while writing code for machine learning applications.

TensorFlow recognizes this and offers abstractions for standard tasks such as data I/O, model building, model evaluation, and model serialization and deserialization out of the box. TF 2.0 systematically organizes these classes of abstractions using two major APIs—Keras and Estimators. These abstractions are very powerful as they enable end users to operate at different levels of detail or sophistication. The following sections will describe both these APIs in detail, and you will learn about the merits and demerits of each and develop an understanding of which APIs to use in what context.

Diving deep into the Keras API

TF 2.0 introduces tighter-than-before coupling with Keras, especially for the high-level APIs. If you are starting out with building neural network-based models in TensorFlow, it is recommended that you start with Keras. In a nutshell, Keras exposes user-friendly APIs for performing common tasks such as loading data, constructing models, training models, evaluating models, running models, and loading and saving previous models. An important factor contributing to its flexibility is that it allows you to seamlessly operate at varying levels of abstraction.

What is Keras?

Keras is a popular high-level API for building and training deep learning models. At its core, Keras is a high-level neural network API specification. It is used extensively in the machine learning community by researchers, hobbyists, and software engineers alike. It was developed with a focus on enabling fast experimentation. It has implementations for a multitude of machine learning platforms and programming languages, such as TensorFlow, MXNet, TypeScript, JavaScript, CNTK, Theano, PlaidML, Python, Scala, and CoreML. TF 2.0 contains a complete implementation of the Keras API specifications with TensorFlow-specific enhancements and optimizations. This is available in the `tf.keras` module.

Keras was built with the explicit design goal of being able to go from idea to results with the least possible delay. The following features make it a good choice for building neural network-based models:

- **Easy and fast model building**: This is largely because of the following reasons:

  - It is an user-friendly API
  - It is modular
  - It is extensible

- **Support for a variety of neural network model architectures**: This includes convolutional networks and recurrent networks, and even combinations of the two
- **Models are hardware agnostic**: Keras models can be run on both CPUs and GPUs without additional code

Building models

Machine learning, at its very core, is a series of statistical computations that are performed to achieve an end goal. These core statistical components can be encapsulated as a model. Furthermore, some standard computations can be viewed as interactions with this core. From a programmer's perspective, it can be useful to look at a model as a black box that contains a bunch of mathematical equations. Then, other actions can be described as a set of interactions with this black box.

For example, **training** a model can be understood as the process of computing parameters (or weights) for a model, given a set of input records. **Inference** can be viewed as a process that uses the mathematical core and learned parameters to generate predictions for a given set of inputs.

Keras roughly adopts the abstraction paradigm that we just discussed to help users to easily build, train, and predict using neural network-based models. In subsequent subsections, we shall look in detail at the options that Keras offers for each one of the aforementioned tasks. We shall also look at other ancillary features that make Keras a powerful force to be reckoned with.

In Keras, models are built using a combination of layers. Each Keras layer roughly corresponds to the layer in the neural network architecture. A model can also be thought of as a combination of layers. Keras offers multiple options to combine these layers to form a neural network-based model. The next two subsections focus on two of the most popular APIs that Keras exposes for building the model, also known as the **mathematical** and **statistical cores**.

The Keras layers API

In the high-level Keras APIs for model building, a Keras layer is the fundamental building block. A **model** is typically defined as some type of graph of these layers. These layers can also be programmed to interact with one another. As these are the fundamental building blocks, we are given the ability to define and customize the behavior of the layers during both the training and inference phases. In other terms, we are given the ability to define the behavior of the layer during both forward and backward passes (if applicable). From a programmer's perspective, a layer can be thought of as a data structure that encapsulates the state, as well as the logic, to generate specific outputs from a given set of inputs.

The layers API is implemented in an object-oriented manner, so as to preserve a uniform interface and encourage code reuse. As a result, all layers have a set of common functions and attributes and some behavior-specific ones. Some examples of common methods are as follows:

- `layer.get_weights()`: This method returns the weights of the layer as a list of NumPy arrays
- `layer.set_weights(weights)`: This method sets the weights of the layer from a list of NumPy arrays (with the same shape as the output of `get_weights`)
- `layer.get_config()`: This method returns a dictionary containing the configuration of the layer

We are also given the flexibility to implement our own custom layers. This is an advanced use case and a detailed discussion would be beyond the scope of the book. If you're interested in this, then you should look up additional resources to this effect. It effectively involves subclassing one or more of the layer classes and adding and modifying functionality.

Some of the common types of layers contained in `tensorflow.keras` include dense layers, convolutional layers, pooling layers, recurrent layers, activation layers, and normalization layers. A variety of generic label wrappers are also made available to enable us to build custom layers.

Let's look at some of the properties of the layers module and see how we can create different types of layers very quickly.

One layer that is common to a high number of neural network architectures is the `Input` layer. This layer works as a placeholder layer to accept inputs from the users. It can be constructed in a very straightforward manner, as shown in the following code block:

```
layer_name = tf.keras.Input(
  shape=None,
  batch_size=None,
  name=None,
  dtype=None,
  sparse=False,
  tensor=None,
  **kwargs
)
```

`tf.keras.layers` contains pre-implemented layers for more sophisticated operations such as regularization, activations, batch normalization, and pooling. Two of the most powerful features include built-in support for recurrent and convolutional architectures. The modular nature of the layers actually enables users to combine both convolutional and recurrent operations in a single network architecture. In subsequent sections, we will see how to create different types of layers and use them in the process of network creation.

Simple model building using the Sequential API

The `Sequential` API is a very simple, yet powerful abstraction that Keras exposes for building models. It is recommended that you use this if you're just starting out with Keras. It is also a recommended option if you are working with single-input stage models.

The primary component of this API is `tf.keras.Sequential`.

This is useful for the simple, serial composition of layers. Let's say you have an *n* layer neural network. Let's say, these layers are defined as `[layer_1, layer_2, .... , layer_n]`.

 Please note that each one of these layers is a Keras layer, as described earlier. For our implementation, this means that the layer object will be one of the layers exposed in `tf.keras.layers` or a user-defined layer subclassing the base Keras layers implementation.

Constituent layers can be combined using the `add()` method of an instance of `tf.keras.Sequential`.

The general form of combining them sequentially is as follows:

```
my_model = tf.keras.Sequential()
my_model.add(layer_1)
.
.
my_model.add(layer_n)
```

Let's say you want to build a model describing a fully connected neural network (also called a **multilayer perceptron (MLP)**) for binary classification of one-dimensional records with five attributes. Our model consists of four fully connected layers. For purely illustrative purposes, let's assume that each fully connected layer contains 10 nodes or neurons. Each one of these layers uses **rectified linear unit (ReLU)** activation functions. The final output is taken over a `softmax` layer. Layer-specific customization can be defined in the constructor for the corresponding layer. The code for implementing this model is as follows:

```
model = tf.keras.Sequential()

# Adds a densely-connected layer with 10 units and rectified linear unit
activations
# Accepts multiple input tensors of size 5 from user
model.add(layers.Dense(10, activation='relu', input_shape=(5,)))

# Add layer 2 with 10 units and relu activations:
model.add(layers.Dense(10, activation='relu'))

# Add layer 3 with 10 units and relu activations:
model.add(layers.Dense(10, activation='relu'))

# Add layer 4 with 10 units and relu activations:
model.add(layers.Dense(10, activation='relu'))
```

```
# Add a softmax layer with 2 output units:
model.add(layers.Dense(2, activation='softmax'))
```

Another way to use the `Sequential` API is to provide all the layers in a list or, in general, as some kind of iterator. These can be passed to the `Sequential()` constructor while initializing the model object. This can be especially useful when separating the layer description and model creation tasks. Let's look at the following examples to understand this better.

Consider the earlier example of trying to generate a model from a list of these layers: `layer_list =[layer_1, layer_2, .... , layer_n]`. The model can now be created by passing the `layer_list` object directly to the constructor, as shown:

```
new_model = tf.keras.Sequential(layer_list)
```

It is worth noting that the preceding statement is equivalent to the following one:

```
new_model = tf.keras.Sequential(layers=layer_list)
```

This can be used in other ways as well. One example would be to separate the layer specification and model creation processes. Let's explore this idea further. Let's say you have a use case where a model requires a number of layers that are only available at runtime.

A simple approach to do this would be to write a function for creating layers. Let's write an example function, `get_layers(n)`, that takes an integer value of n and returns the many `Dense` layers one after the other. To illustrate the flexibility of the API, let's implement the function using Python generators:

```
def get_layers(n):
    while n > 0:
        yield tf.keras.Dense(10, activation='relu')
        n -= 1
```

 If you are not familiar with Python generators, please refer to `https://realpython.com/introduction-to-python-generators/` before proceeding.

The function defined in the preceding code block accepts a positive integer value of n and returns a `generator` object. Each element produced by this generator is a layer. The following code snippet shows how we can use this function to create a model:

```
model_using_generator = tf.keras.Sequential(layers=get_layers(10))
```

Advanced model building using the functional API

As machine learning tasks grow in sophistication, models with multi-stage inputs and outputs become increasingly common. A sizable chunk of real-world use cases involve models with multi-stage inputs and outputs. An example of a real-world model with multiple inputs is a text classification model that looks at both words and character sequences in the input text.

While the Sequential API does a very good job of combining layers in a serial fashion, it cannot be used for describing parallel compositions of underlying layers. In general, it cannot be used to build layer graphs that do not have a linear topology. Its utility is also restricted in cases when a particular layer needs to be utilized multiple times, either within the same model or across models. This is why the functional API becomes necessary.

The functional API leverages the idea that individual layers are callable on other tensors. This makes it possible to chain different layers and tensors together in non-linear topologies. To create such a link between two layers, they would need to be combined in some way. This is done by calling the current layer and passing the previous layer as an argument. For example, a sample link of layer_1 -> layer_2 (where layer_1 and layer_2 are Keras layers) can be created as follows:

```
layer_1 = tf.keras.Input(shape=(10, ))
layer_2 = tf.keras.layers.Dense(20)

# Creating link
linked_layer_2 = layer_2(layer_1)
```

To demonstrate the creation of non-linear network topologies, consider the structures of layer_2 and layer_3, which are created from a common layer, layer_1:

```
layer_1 = tf.keras.Input(shape=(10, ))

layer_2 = tf.keras.layers.Dense(10)
layer_2 = layer_2(layer_1)

layer_3 = tf.keras.layers.Dense(10) (layer_1)
layer_3 = layer_3(layer_1)
```

The preceding code can be equivalently written, as shown in the following code block. This transformation uses a smaller number of lines and is much more intuitive and readable:

```
layer_1 = tf.keras.Input(shape=(10, ))
layer_2 = tf.keras.layers.Dense(10)(layer_1)
layer_3 = tf.keras.layers.Dense(10)(layer_1)
```

Once we have chained the independent layers together as needed, it becomes important to define the actual model. To do so, we need to define the input and output layers or tensors. For a model with n different input layers and m output layers, the general way of doing this is shown in the following code block:

```
model = tf.keras.Model(
            inputs=[input_layer_1, .., input_layer_n],
            outputs=[output_layer_1, ..,output_layer_m]
        )
```

Adapting this to the preceding non-linear topology example, let's use a model with one input (layer_1) and two outputs (layer_2 and layer_3):

```
# Define layers and their interactions
layer_1 = tf.keras.Input(shape=(10, ))
layer_2 = tf.keras.layers.Dense(10)(layer_1)
layer_3 = tf.keras.layers.Dense(10)(layer_1)

# Build Model
sample_non_linear_model = tf.keras.Model(
                            inputs=[layer_1],
                            outputs=[layer_2, layer_3]
                        )
```

Let's try to apply what we've learned so far to recreate the same neural network built in the Sequential API section using the functional API. As you may recall, we created a fully connected neural network for binary classification of one-dimensional records with five attributes. Our model consists of four fully connected layers. For purely illustrative purposes, let's assume that each fully connected layer contains 10 nodes or neurons. Each one of these layers uses the relu activation function. The final output is taken over a softmax layer. The code for implementing this model by using the functional API is as follows:

```
input_layer = tf.keras.Input(shape=(5, ))

# Adds a densely-connected layer with 10 units and Rectified Linear (relu)
activations
# Accepts multiple input tensors of size 5 from user
output_layer = layers.Dense(10, activation='relu')(input_layer)
```

```
# Add layer 2 with 10 units and relu activations:
output_layer = layers.Dense(10, activation='relu')(output_layer)
# Add layer 2 with 10 units and relu activations:
output_layer = layers.Dense(10, activation='relu')(output_layer)

# Add layer 3 with 10 units and relu activations:
output_layer = layers.Dense(10, activation='relu')(output_layer)

# Add layer 4 with 10 units and relu activations:_
output_layer = layers.Dense(10, activation='relu')(output_layer)

# Add a softmax layer with 2 output units:
output_layer = layers.Dense(2, activation='softmax')(output_layer)

# Create a model by specifying inputs and outputs
model = tf.keras.Model(
            inputs=[input_layer],
            outputs=[output_layer]
        )
```

Training models

Training a model refers to the process of learning weights for different network components that minimize the loss function over a given set of examples. In simpler terms, training a neural network means finding the best combination of values for the network. As you might know, the training process is very closely linked to the evaluation and prediction process as well. Leveraging the power of abstractions, Keras provides powerful high-level interfaces to implement and manage the training process from end to end. Let's look at the training API it offers for models created using the sequential and functional APIs. Some of the functions that it offers for this phase are discussed as follows:

- `model.compile()`: This function is used to configure the training process. Users specify details such as the type of optimizer (and hyperparameters, if any), the type of loss function, and metrics to evaluate. These are also the same metrics that can be visualized using TensorBoard. The following sample snippet describes a sample training configuration with a **stochastic gradient descent** (**SGD**) optimizer, the `CategoricalCrossentropy` loss function, and the record `Accuracy` metric:

```
model.compile(
            # Optimizer
            optimizer=tf.keras.optimizers.SGD(),

            # Loss function to minimize
```

```
            loss=keras.losses.CategoricalCrossentropy(),

            # List of metrics to monitor
            metrics=[
                    keras.metrics.SparseCategoricalAccuracy()
            ]
)
```

- `model.fit()`: This method is used to provide training data and control the actual training process. Some of the important parameters and arguments that go into this method are training records, training labels, number of training epochs, and training batch size. The following sample snippet describes a sample training process for training a predefined model for 30 epochs, with a batch size of 32, on training records (`train_x`) and training labels (`train_y`):

```
model.fit(
        x=train_x,
        y=train_y,
        epochs=30,
        batch_size=32
)
```

- `model.evaluate()`: As discussed earlier, the training and evaluation processes are interlinked and very closely coupled. Training a neural network involves frequently updating the weights to find the best possible set of weights. To do this, it is necessary to compute some type of state of the network at the current stage. This process is known as **evaluation**. In more detailed terms, evaluation is the process of computing the loss and other metrics of the network at the current stage for the given dataset. Please keep in mind that the computation performed by this method is performed in batches. This function returns a scalar corresponding to the loss function. It also returns the values corresponding to any metrics provided in the `model.compile()` phase. The following snippet describes an evaluation function that computes metrics on records (`test_x`) and labels (`test_y`), with a batch size of 32:

```
results = model.evaluate(
        test_x,
        test_y,
        batch_size=32
    )
```

Saving and loading models

After training, it can be extremely useful to save the model for later use. Decoupling the training and inference pipelines is a good idea in many use cases. From a developer's perspective, a model can be abstracted out as a black box that accepts a set of inputs and returns some outputs. Saving a model, then, is nothing but exporting an artifact that represents this black box. Restoring or loading models then becomes the process of using this black box to perform some real work. This can also be understood as the process of **serializing** and **deserializing** the model black box.

TF 2.0 supports saving and restoring a model in multiple modes:

- Model architecture only (Keras)
- Model weights only (Keras)
- The entire model:
    - Using Keras
    - Using `SavedModel`

TF 2.0 standardizes `SavedModel` as the primary model-exchange approach. This is done to ensure that models can be freely used across different platforms such as TensorFlow Lite, TensorFlow Mobile, TensorFlow.js, TensorFlow Edge, TensorBoard, TensorHub, and TensorServing.

In this section, we will learn how to load and save models created with the `Sequential` and `functional` APIs. It is important for readers to understand that these techniques do not work for models created using other model creation approaches.

Saving a model refers to the process of serializing the model (or parts of it) in memory and storing it on disk (or some other storage medium). This is helpful in recording the current state of the model and using it at a later time and probably in a different environment. **Loading a model** is the inverse of the saving process. It refers to the process of reconstructing the model in memory from a serialized representation. It, in other words, is the process of deserialization.

Loading and saving architecture and weights separately

In some use cases, it makes sense to decouple the model creation and model initialization steps. In such scenarios, model serialization would necessitate having separate processes for loading and saving architectures and model weights. Keras offers support for users to independently work with the architectures and weights.

Loading and saving architectures

In the `tf.Keras` Python API, the fundamental unit for architecture interchange is a Python `dict`. Keras models use the `get_config()` method to generate this `dict` from an existing model. This `dict` can then be saved to disk or any other storage medium using standard Python serialization and deserialization approaches such as Pickle or HD5. You can also directly write the Python `dict` to a file on disk.

Let's say you want to save the architecture of a Keras model, `my_model`, to disk. The following snippet illustrates how to do this:

```
my_model_architecture = my_model.get_config()
```

You can now save this Python `dict` to disk using your approach of choice.

For the inverse use case of generating a model from a config object, Keras uses the `from_config()` method. It is possible to recreate the architecture of a model at a later stage and in a different environment using the Python dictionary created in the previous stage. To do so, simply load the Python `dict` into memory and use it to create a Keras model, as shown in the following code block:

```
replica_my_model = keras.Model.from_config(my_model_architecture)
```

Loading and saving weights

In the Python API, `tensorflow.keras` uses NumPy arrays as the unit of exchanging weights. This is very similar to the API for loading and saving architectures. These NumPy arrays can also be saved to disk using native Python techniques. The `get_weights()` and `set_weights()` methods are roughly analogous to `get_config()` and `from_config()`. The former returns a list of NumPy arrays corresponding to the different layers in the model. The latter accepts a list of NumPy arrays and updates the model in memory.

The following snippet illustrates how to get the weights of an existing model:

```
my_model_weights = my_model.get_weights()
```

Given a set of weights and a model replica, the inverse operation of updating the weights of the model in memory can be performed as follows:

```
replica_my_model.set_weights(my_model_weights)
```

As we can see, it is possible to store an entire model using a combination of `get_config()` or `get_weights()` with `from_config` or `set_weights()`. A limitation of this process, though, is that it doesn't store any information about the training process.

To understand this better, let's look at an example. Consider a simple model with one input layer, one hidden layer, and one output layer. We will then create a replica of this model by exclusively using the methods discussed in the preceding section. The following are the steps:

1. To get started, let's define this model using the `functional` API:

```
# Define layer chain
input_layer = tf.keras.layers.Input(shape=(5,))
hidden_layer = tf.keras.layers.Dense(10)(input_layer)
output_layer = tf.keras.layers.Dense(5,
activation='softmax')(hidden_layer)

# Define Model
my_model = tf.keras.Model(inputs=input_layer, outputs=output_layer)
```

2. The goal here is to create a replica of the preceding model. To do this, let's create copies of the model's architecture and the model's weights:

```
# Save architecture
my_model_arch = my_model.get_config()

# Save weights
my_model_weights = my_model.get_weights()
```

3. To create our replica model, we have to create a Keras model with an architecture identical to the source model:

```
# Create replica using saved architecture
my_model_replica = tf.keras.Model.from_config(my_model_arch)
```

4. Next, we copy the weights from the source model to the model copy:

```
# Copy saved weights
my_model_replica.set_weights(
    my_model_weights
)
```

As you can see, we have successfully created a copy of the source model using the save API. Furthermore, we've tested this by loading it back into a separate object memory using the load APIs described earlier. In other words, we've created a copy of the model using the load and save APIs.

Saving and loading entire models

One of the major limitations of the process described in the preceding section is that it doesn't include the training process. This can be a major impediment in use cases that involve checkpointing at some point during the training process. To overcome it, TensorFlow makes it possible to save models in their entirety. This can primarily be achieved in two ways—using the Keras API or using the `SavedModel` API.

In the following sections, we briefly discuss both methods and their syntax. We also provide insights into when to use each.

Using Keras

It is possible to save models built with the `Sequential` API or the `functional` API in a single file. It is also possible to load this very model from this file, independent of the code used to build the model.

This file includes the following:

- The model's architecture
- The model's weight values (including the ones learned during training, if applicable)
- The optimizer and its state, if any (can be used to resume training from a particular point)
- The model's training config (which was passed to compile), if any

Keras models created using the `Sequential` or `functional` APIs can be directly saved to disk. The files are saved using Keras' native HDF5 file format. The general form of the code to achieve this is as follows:

```
model.save('file_name.h5')
```

This model can be reloaded into memory using a simple Python one-liner. The general format is as follows:

```
loaded_model = tf.keras.models.load_model(
                                    'path_to_model.h5'
                                    )
```

This is a very straightforward approach that works well when exchanging models within the Python API.

Using the SavedModel API

SavedModel is the default way of storing objects in the TensorFlow ecosystem. Owing to this standardized nature, it can be used to exchange models across different TensorFlow implementations. Models saved using SavedModel contain actual TensorFlow code in addition to the model architectures and weights. The exact contents of the SavedModel files can be listed as follows:

- A TensorFlow checkpoint containing the model weights
- A SavedModel proto containing the underlying TensorFlow graph:
  - Separate graphs are saved for the prediction phase by default (the training and evaluation phases are also stored as and when applicable)
- The model's architecture configuration (if any)

In the Python API, interacting with SavedModel is very straightforward. The tf.saved_model module provides two appropriately named methods, load() and save(), to load a model from disk and save a model to disk.

For this example, we have a Keras model named my_model that was created using the functional and Sequential APIs. To save it in a folder on disk using SavedModel, we can use the following snippet:

```
tf.saved_model.save(
                    my_model,
                    "path_to_folder_on_disk"
                    )
```

Similarly, to load a model into memory from disk, we can use the following:

```
loaded_model = tf.saved_model.load(
                                    "path_to_folder"
                    )
```

While the preceding snippets only cover the Python API, please keep in mind that models saved using SavedModel are API-agnostic, which means that they are independent of the code and even the programming language used to create them! This makes it possible for SavedModel to be utilized across the TensorFlow ecosystem.

Other features

In addition to a very powerful API specification, TensorFlow's `tf.keras` Keras implementation comes with a bunch of additional add-ons. We will briefly discuss two of the most relevant ones in the following sections.

The keras.applications module

The `keras.applications` module contains pre-built architectures with weights for popular models. These can be used directly for making predictions. Users may also use them to create input features for other networks. Prominent prebuilt implementations in the package include the following:

- `densenet module`: A DenseNet model for Keras
- `inception_resnet_v2`: An Inception-ResNet V2 model for Keras
- `inception_v3`: An Inception V3 model for Keras
- `mobilenet`: A MobileNet v1 model for Keras
- `mobilenet_v2`: A MobileNet v2 model for Keras
- `nasnet`: A NASNet-A model for Keras
- `resnet50`: A ResNet50 model for Keras
- `vgg16`: A VGG16 model for Keras
- `vgg19`: A VGG19 model for Keras
- `xception`: An Xception V1 model for Keras

> Each one of the preceding models is a Python module. A detailed description of the API and the components of each of the modules is available at `https://www.tensorflow.org/versions/r2.0/api_docs/python/tf/keras/applications`.

The keras.datasets module

The `keras.datasets` module includes automation to parse data from files for certain popular datasets. It also includes automation to download these files over the internet if they aren't available locally. This makes it easier and faster for users to experiment with and evaluate different models. For certain use cases, this module can replace the entire data processing stage! The various dataset modules that come with Keras include the following:

- `boston_housing`: The Boston housing price regression dataset
- `cifar10`: The CIFAR10 small images classification dataset
- `cifar100`: The CIFAR100 small images classification dataset
- `fashion_mnist`: The fashion-MNIST dataset
- `imdb`: The IMDB sentiment classification dataset
- `mnist`: The MNIST handwritten digits dataset
- `reuters`: The Reuters topic classification dataset

 Each one of the listed datasets is a Python module. A detailed list of its components is available at `https://www.tensorflow.org/versions/r2.0/api_docs/python/tf/keras/datasets`.

An end-to-end Sequential example

Let's now use the components of the Keras API that we discussed in the preceding section for a small real-world task. Let's build a neural network using the `Sequential` API for classifying handwritten digits from the MNIST dataset. The steps are as follows:

1. Before we can start writing any functional code, we need to import `tensorflow` and `keras` into memory:

    ```
    import tensorflow as tf
    import tensorflow.keras as keras
    ```

2. Then, let's get started by loading the dataset into memory. To do this, let's use the `keras.datasets` module, as discussed in earlier sections:

    ```
    # Load Data
    (x_train, y_train), (x_test, y_test) =
    keras.datasets.mnist.load_data()
    ```

3. In the preceding snippet, the data is loaded into memory as numpy arrays. Let's convert the records to TensorFlow tensors before using them:

```
# Convert records from numpy arrays to tensors
x_train = tf.convert_to_tensor(
    x_train,
    dtype='float'
)

x_test = tf.convert_to_tensor(
    x_test,
    dtype='float'
)
```

4. Also, the labels are loaded as numpy arrays with integer values. Let's convert them to tensors with one-hot representation:

```
# Convert integer labels to one-hot encoded Tensors
y_train = tf.one_hot(
    y_train,
    depth=10
)

y_test = tf.one_hot(
    y_test,
    depth=10
)
```

All of our data is now successfully represented as tensors. Each record currently is a 28 x 28 image. Each label is a one-hot encoded tensor of size 10. We will be using a fully connected neural network to perform classification.

5. Then, initialize the model using the Sequential API:

```
# Build neural network for classification
model = keras.Sequential()
```

6. As our records are currently two-dimensional, we declare an Input layer that flattens out the record. To do this, we use the Flatten layer from tf.keras.layers:

```
# Flatten records before feeding to the network
model.add(
    keras.layers.Flatten()
)
```

Our input is now in the desired format.

7. Let's define a network structure to perform the classification. We start with defining two hidden layers with `100` nodes each and some `relu` activations:

```
# Define the hidden layers of the model
model.add(
    keras.layers.Dense(100,
                        activation='relu',
                        )
)
model.add(
    keras.layers.Dense(100,
                        activation='relu'
                        )
)
```

8. Lastly, we take outputs over a `softmax` layer with `10` nodes:

```
model.add(
    keras.layers.Dense(10,
                        activation='softmax')
)
```

At this stage, we have successfully defined the different layers of our model.

9. We now need to codify the training process using the `model.compile()` method. We will use the SGD optimizer along with `categorical_crossentropy` as the loss function. We would also like to keep track of the accuracy metric during the training process:

```
# Compile model
model.compile(loss=keras.losses.categorical_crossentropy,
              optimizer=keras.optimizers.SGD(),
              metrics=['accuracy'])
```

10. Let's now train the model on our training data. We use a batch size of `32` and run the training for `10` epochs:

```
# Train model
model.fit(x_train,
          y_train,
          batch_size=32,
          epochs=10)
```

11. Finally, we run an evaluation on the model:

```
# Run evaluation
score = model.evaluate(x_test,
                       y_test
                       )
print('Test loss:', score[0])
print('Test accuracy:', score[1])
```

You should see something similar to the following output:

```
Test loss: 0.18730500682010315
Test accuracy: 0.9491
```

As you can see, we've managed to train a model that manages to achieve an accuracy of 94%. We've thus seen how easy it is to implement and experiment with neural networks using `tf.Keras`.

Estimators

When building machine learning models from the ground up, a practitioner would typically go through a number of high-level stages. These include training, evaluation, prediction, and shipping for use at scale (or exporting). Until now, developers have had to write custom code to implement each one of these steps. A lot of the boilerplate code necessary to run these processes remains the same across applications. To make things worse, this code can easily necessitate operating at low levels of abstraction. These issues, when put together, can become a huge inefficiency in the development process.

The TensorFlow team attempted to fix this problem by introducing Estimators, a high-level API that aims to abstract out a lot of the complexities incurred whilst performing different tasks in the aforementioned phases. Specifically, Estimators are a high-level API used to encapsulate tasks in the following categories:

- Training
- Evaluation
- Prediction
- Model sharing (exporting and shipping models)

Users can choose from a set of pre-built Estimators or even implement their own. Implementations of Estimators for a variety of commonly used machine learning and deep learning algorithms are available in the standard library.

Estimators provide the following benefits:

- Estimator-based models are hardware- and environment-agnostic:
  - The programmer doesn't have to care about whether the Estimator is running on their local machine or on a remote computing grid.
  - Programmers can run Estimator-based models on CPUs, GPUs, or TPUs without recoding their model.
- Estimators simplify sharing implementations across developers on a team or between teams using different environments or stacks.
- Programmers can develop high-performance and cutting-edge models with high-level intuitive code. In other words, the programmer doesn't have to waste time on managing the complexities of the low-level TensorFlow APIs.
- Estimators are built on `tf.keras.layers` themselves, which simplifies customization.
- Estimators build the graph for you.
- Estimators provide a safely distributed training loop that controls how and when to perform the following:
  - Building the graph
  - Initializing variables
  - Loading data
  - Handling exceptions
  - Creating checkpoint files and recovering from failures
  - Saving summaries for TensorBoard
- When writing an application with Estimators, programmers have the flexibility to separate the data input pipeline from the model. This separation makes it easy to experiment with different datasets and different data sources.

In TF 2.0, a lot of the functionality exposed by Estimators is already served by Keras. If you are just starting out, Keras is an easier API to learn. It is recommended that beginners use Keras APIs over Estimators. Once your use case necessitates using Estimators, you may look it up and learn more. A detailed guide is available at: `https://www.tensorflow.org/guide/estimators`.

Evaluating TensorFlow graphs

The central idea of TensorFlow used to be that the programmer was required to create a compute graph to specify the operations that need to be performed to achieve the desired result. Programmers then specified the hardware and other environmental parameters to compute the output of this compute graph for a given set of inputs. This meant that the values and variables didn't have any values until the graph was explicitly computed by the programmers. This added overhead for programmers to create and manage sessions when all they really wanted was the value of the quantity.

TF 2.0 aims to solve this issue by making changes to the way the underlying compute graph is evaluated and computed. In a single sentence, TF 2.0 now uses **eager execution**, as compared to lazy loading in lower versions. The following sections describe these terms in detail. We also highlight what these mean to end users and how the new changes can be leveraged to do more with less code.

Lazy loading versus eager execution

Lazy loading is a programming paradigm where the value of a quantity is not computed until the quantity is actually needed. In other words, an object isn't initialized until it is explicitly requested. The major benefit of this is that as values of quantities are computed on demand, no additional memory is used to store computed results. If used correctly, this can lead to very efficient usage of memory and can also improve speeds.

Eager execution can be understood to be the opposite of lazy loading. Here, the value of the quantity is computed as soon as it is defined, without waiting until it is called. This means that when the quantity is actually requested, the value is returned from memory instead of being computed from scratch. This helps minimize the time it takes to return the result of a query, as the user doesn't have to wait for the time taken to compute the value.

The difference between both can be illustrated using a simple operation of adding two constants: *a* and *b*. First, let's look at the versions of TensorFlow before 2.0. These required the user to define a compute graph and then use sessions to run and evaluate the graph. This can be understood as an example of lazy loading. Let's look at the following snippet to get a better idea:

```
# Define constants
a = tf.constant(10)
b = tf.constant(32)


# Define add operation
```

```
c = a + b
print(f"Value outside session: {c}")
```

This gives the following output:

Outside session: Tensor("add_1:0", shape=(), dtype=int32)

At this stage, we can see that the value of c—that is, the result of the add operation on two constants—is actually a tensor with no actual numerical value. Thus, we can see that the graph has been constructed but not yet evaluated. In order to get the actual numerical result of the add operation, we would have to define a session to run and evaluate the underlying graph:

```
# Create a session and run graph in it
with tf.Session() as sess:
  print(f"Value inside Session: {c}")
```

You will see the following output:

Value inside Session: 42

This shows that the add operation was evaluated only after it was run in a session.

Now, let's try the same example with TF 2.0 and higher. We define the two constants with the same variable names and values. We also define a third variable to hold the result of the addition. We then print the value of the addition immediately after:

```
# Define constants
a = tf.constant(10)
b = tf.constant(32)

#Define add operation
c = a + b
print(f"Value outside session: {c}")
```

The resultant output is as follows:

Value outside session: 42

As we can see, the outputs at this stage are different between TensorFlow versions 2.0+ and <2.0. In this case, the variable of c already contains the value of the add operation. This was computed without the programmer having to evaluate any compute graphs. In other words, the add operation was eagerly executed. This is the primary difference between 2.0+ and older versions.

TF 2.0 is tightly integrated with the Python programming language. Eager execution enables seamless use of tensors as native Python objects without having to worry about evaluating compute graphs and managing sessions or underlying hardware. The benefits don't end here. Eager execution enables programmers to leverage the powerful control flow structures of the host programming language. This adds a huge amount of value for developers as TensorFlow code now integrates much more intuitively with the rest of the platform, because it no longer requires special flow-control structures. This also adds significant value for experimentation, debugging, and notebook environments.

Summary

In this chapter, we have learned about the high-level abstractions available in TF 2.0 for model building, training, saving, and loading. Diving deep into the Keras API, we learned about how to build models by combining layers using the `Sequential` and `functional` APIs. We have also learned about how to leverage the high-level abstractions of the Keras API for training models. The chapter also looked at the intricacies of loading and saving models in various configurations and modes. We have learned about different methods of saving models, architectures, and weights, and this chapter presented an in-depth explanation of each approach and described when you should pick one over the other.

Putting together all the concepts discussed, the chapter outlined an end-to-end example program to build and train models using the Keras `Sequential` API. It also provided a brief overview of Estimators and how they compare to the Keras API.

This chapter also looked at the change in the evaluation of the underlying compute graph from lazy loading to eager execution. Briefly introducing the concepts of lazy loading and eager execution, this chapter went into detail about how programming in TF 2.0 is different from earlier versions. Through hands-on examples, we learned about the practical ramifications of the change discussed earlier and how to deal with them in real-life situations.

In the next chapter, we will learn how to design and construct input data pipelines.

2

Section 2: TensorFlow 2.0 - Data and Model Training Pipelines

This section of the book will outline the overall input data and the training model pipeline. It will also detail model creation using `tf.keras` APIs, training, and the validation flow.

This section contains the following chapters:

3
Designing and Constructing Input Data Pipelines

This chapter will give an overview of how to build complex input data pipelines for ingesting large training/inference datasets in the most common formats, such as CSV files, images, text, and so on using `tf.data` APIs consisting of the `TFRecords` and `tf.data.Dataset` methods. You will also get a general idea about protocol buffers, protocol messages, and how they are implemented using the `TFRecords` and `tf.Example` methods in **TensorFlow 2.0 (TF 2.0)**. This chapter also explains the best practices for using the `tf.data.Dataset` method with respect to the shuffling, batching, and prefetching of data, and provides recommendations in terms of TF 2.0. Finally, we will talk about the built-in TensorFlow datasets, which have been newly added and are extremely useful for building a prototype model training pipeline.

The following topics will be covered in this chapter:

- Designing and constructing the data pipeline
- Transforming datasets
- Feeding the created dataset to the model
- Examples of complete end-to-end data pipelines
- Best practices and the performance optimization of a data pipeline in TF 2.0
- Built-in datasets in TF 2.0

Technical requirements

You should know about standard data formats such as CSV files, images (PNG and JPG), and ASCII text formats. Needless to say, most of the chapters in this book assume that you know about basic machine learning concepts, Python programming, the numpy Python module, and that you have used TensorFlow to create some machine learning models. Though it's not required, having familiarity with tf.data APIs from **TensorFlow 1.x (TF 1.x)** versions will be helpful. Even if you don't have prior knowledge of tf.data APIs, you should find this chapter self-sufficient to learn about them.

Some of the topics in this chapter require Python modules such as argparse and tqdm, which are listed on this book's GitHub repository. The code for this chapter is available at https://github.com/PacktPublishing/What-s-New-in-TensorFlow-2.0/tree/master/Chapter03.

Designing and constructing the data pipeline

One of the most important requirements when it comes to training **machine learning (ML)** models and **deep neural networks (DNNs)** is having large training datasets with distributions (mostly unknown, which we learn about during ML or DNN training) from a given sample space so that ML models and DNNs can learn from this given training data and generalize well to unseen future or separated out test data. Also, a validation dataset, which often comes from the same source as the training set distribution, is critical to fine-tuning model hyperparameters. In many cases, developers start with whatever data is available—either a little or a lot—to train machine learning models, including high capacity deep neural networks. Regardless of the data's size and format, it is important to feed training, validation, and test data to TensorFlow models in an efficient manner so that training runtime is optimized. To achieve this, TensorFlow provides great support by using tf.data APIs. Using tf.data APIs (more specifically, tf.data.Dataset), you can stream training, validation, and test data from disk in a seamless and efficient manner for model training and inferencing.

This is one of the differences from TensorFlow versions that are older than 2.0. In TF 1.x, `feed_dict` was used, along with the regular Python iteration and generators. For more complex input data ingestion, the `QueueRunner` API was used. The `tf.data` set of APIs in TF 2.0 have simplified and removed a lot of complexity in the code by removing the need for `feed_dict`, `QueueRunner`, and other complicated constructs. In this chapter, we will design, prepare, and construct the data pipeline.

In data mining, one of the most popular procedures for managing data from one or multiple sources into a target system is **extract, transform, load** (**ETL**). The ETL technique involves three distinct steps, as its name suggests. A typical `tf.data.Dataset`-based input pipeline is based on the following ETL principle:

- Extract raw data from multiple persistent sources. These sources could be either local disks or over a distributed network.
- Transform data to parse, preprocess, augment, shuffle, and batch it.
- Load the transformed data to devices such as GPUs and TPUs to run ML model training and inference.

Also, clean training data is essential to train an ML model in order to achieve good results from the model (to avoid the famous garbage in, garbage out issue (which can be seen at https://en.wikipedia.org/wiki/Garbage_in,_garbage_out)). Input data needs to be collected (extracted—the E of ETL), preprocessed, cleaned, and normalized (transformed—the T of ETL) before being fed into the ML model. Afterward, the data needs to be fed into (loaded—the L of ETL) the model to train. The `tf.data` API provides a rich set of APIs that you can use to design and construct superior ETL-based input pipelines, it offers easy ways to fetch data, and to transform data for data augmentation, and for normalization purposes through its transformation APIs, which are loaded into TensorFlow models.

During the remainder of this chapter, we will take a deep dive and show you how the ETL technique is used to build a data pipeline.

The `tf.data` API can handle a variety of data formats, such as text, CSV, images, videos, and so on, which can be efficiently ingested. It can be used with TensorFlow model creation APIs such as `tf.keras` and `tf.Estimators`, and even with low-level APIs. However, one of the recommendations in TF 2.0 is to use `tf.keras` APIs as extensively as possible. It's noteworthy that, for advanced users who want to use lower-level APIs to build their models, `tf.keras` model subclassing can be used (this will be explained in `Chapter 4`, *Model Training and Use of TensorBoard*, in great detail).

We will start with suggestive block-level diagrams so that we can design and construct the input data pipeline, which is based on the ETL principle, and go deeper into each of the blocks and explain them along the way. A machine or deep learning engineer can follow either of the pipelines that are shown on the left-hand side of the following diagram:

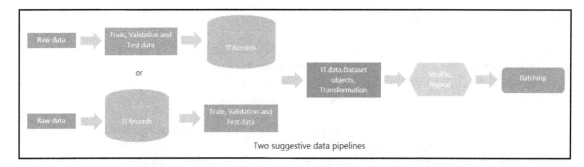

Two suggestive data pipelines

A practical recommendation would be to follow the following flow; however, which one you choose depends on what structure your data is in:

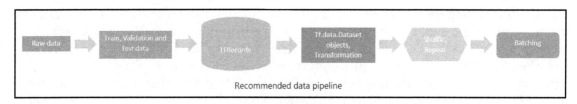

Recommended data pipeline

In the preceding diagram, starting from the raw data, we split the data into train, validation, and test data, and create sets of **TFRecords** files, which are binary storage files saved on disk. Furthermore, **tf.data.Dataset objects** are created and the required transformations into dataset objects are done, such as feature transformation and data augmentation. Once dataset objects have been created and transformed, they need to be shuffled and repeated for training purposes, followed by the batching of the data so that it can be added to the ML model further.

Let's go ahead and look at the individual pieces of the preceding flow one by one and build the overall pipeline.

Raw data

Raw data, which is used to train an ML model, can be text files, CSV files, images, videos, or custom formatted files. Raw data can even be a combination of these file types. Raw data can also be sequenced data, such as time series data—alternatively, it can even be vector representations for text, such as word embeddings. It's important to ensure that the raw input data is managed before it's fed into the model since it can affect the efficiency of the model's training at runtime.

In many cases, raw data can be stored in a database, such as MySQL, MS SQL, MongoDB, and so on. For the sake of this book, it's assumed that even tabular, SQL, or NoSQL data is raw data and that it needs to be split and converted into `TFRecords` for machine/deep learning model purposes. Explaining SQL and NoSQL databases is beyond the scope of this book.

Splitting data into train, validation, and test data

One of the key features of data preparation for ML model training is to be able to split existing data into train, validation, and test sets. Train data is the data that is seen and used to fit or train the model; for example, the learning weights and biases of a neural network. Validation data (sometimes referred to as development data) is used to fine-tune the hyperparameters of the model, such as the learning rate, which optimizer to use, and so on. A model sees this data on a frequent basis (for example, after every iteration or epoch) and evaluates the model.

Please note that validation data just helps you fine-tune the model; it doesn't update weights and bias.

Lastly, test data is the only data that a model never sees at training time (at least, it shouldn't). Test data is used to see how well the model performed on the test data. The following diagram shows the flow of splitting raw data into train, validation, and test data:

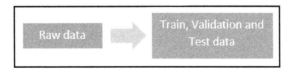

Typically, the data is split into train, validation, and test data; in some cases, it's just split into train and validation data, where the test data is provided separately or is used as future data. Regardless, we assume that developers need to split their raw data into these three types. Data splitting is crucial to successfully train any model, and works well for test or inference data. As good practice, engineers typically follow an 80/10/10 (percentages) split for train, validation, and test data when the total available data size is low (less than 100,000); however, if the data's size is in the range of millions, the split can be either 96/2/2 (percentage) or 98/1/1 (percentage), respectively, as shown in the following diagram:

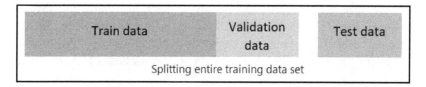

Splitting entire training data set

The idea is to keep a sufficient amount of validation and test data from the entire set of available data, depending on your model's capacity—such as the number of parameters and hyperparameters. For example, if a model is a deep neural network with many layers and neuron units in each layer, you need to have a larger validation set. Also, this split should be so that the validation and test data yields a meaningful representation of data distribution. One such working strategy is to have these splits stochastic and random. In many cases, test data is curated by experts to ensure that various samples of classification classes are available from future real-world data as test data.

There are various ways to split raw data into these three types, and which one should be used is dependent on the preference of the developer. The following are some references on how to split data, for the sake of completeness:

Please note that data scientists use various methods for the split.

- **Using scikit-learn**: The Python `scikit-learn` module provides a function, `sklearn.model_selection.train_test_split(...)`, which can be used to split a given dataset into train, validation, and test sets, as follows:

```
# code shows splitting data to train, validation and test using
sklearn
# Example from
https://stackoverflow.com/questions/38250710/how-to-split-data-into
-3-sets-train-validation-and-test

val_data_size = 10
test_data_size = 10
train_data, rest_data =
    sklearn.model_selection.train_test_split(entire_data,
    test_size=(val_data_size + test_data_size))

new_test_data_size =
    np.around(test_data_size / (val_data_size + test_data_size), 2)
# new_val_data_size
new_val_data_size = 1.0 - new_test_data_size

val_data, test_data =
    sklearn.model_selection.train_test_split(rest_data,
    test_size=new_test_data_size)
```

- **Using Python NumPy**: The Python `numpy` module also provides various ways to split data. The following is one such way:

```
# code shows splitting data to train, validation and test using
numpy
# split(...) function from a panda's Dataframe
# Example from
https://stackoverflow.com/questions/38250710/how-to-split-data-into
-3-sets-train-validation-and-test/

val_data_size = 10
test_data_size = 10
val_offset = 0.8
test_offset = 0.9
df = pandas.Dataframe(entire_data)
train_data, val_data, test_data =
    np.split(df.sample(frac=1), [int(val_offset*len(df)),
    int(test_offset*len(df))])
```

Creating TFRecords

The creation of TFRecords is core to the input data pipeline so that you can create a `tf.data.Dataset` object. It's worth noting that you can create datasets directly using raw data, without the creation of **TFRecords** (which will be explained in the next section). However, the recommended way is to create **TFRecords** from raw (split) data first and then use it for the dataset pipeline. This is a key part of TF 2.0's input data pipeline design. The following diagram shows the flow of the creation of **TFRecords**:

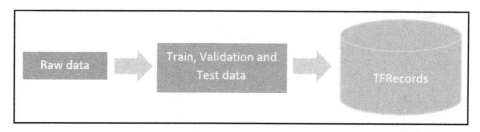

TFRecords help us read data efficiently by serializing data to disk, and can be stored in a set of **TFRecords** files. The recommended size of each file is 100 MB to 200 MB each. It should be noted that `TFRecord` is a binary format that can store any kind of data. As it's a binary format, it takes less disk space, as well as taking less time to copy or read from disk storage. **TFRecords** are also required when it comes to training data that's too large to be stored in in-memory servers, GPUs, and/or TPUs. Using **TFRecords** with datasets, the data can be loaded on an on-demand basis from disk in the form of batches (which will be explained a bit later in this chapter, in the *Batching* section).

There are four important components of `TFRecords`:

- `TFRecord` formats, which are used to store a sequence of binary records or data.
- Protocol buffers (`https://developers.google.com/protocol-buffers/`) are cross-platform and have a cross-language library for the efficient serialization of structured data in the form of protocol messages.
- Protocol messages are small, logical records of information that contain a series of name-value pairs.
- `tf.Example` is a flexible protocol message (also known as `protobuf`) that's designed to be used with TensorFlow. **TensorFlow Extended** (**TFX**) is another great feature in TF 2.0 that's used to deploy production-level ML pipelines, which we will learn about in `Chapter 5`, *Model Inference Pipelines – Multi-platform Deployments*.

Please note that, in TF 2.0, `tf.Examples` have been used throughout high-level APIs such as TFX (`https://www.tensorflow.org/tfx/`).

Now, let's see how the data is stored in `TFRecords`. As we mentioned previously, any data that is converted into `TFRecords` format is stored as a sequence of binary strings. As you might guess, the structure of the data has to be specified upfront before you can read or write from `tfrecord` files. In order to read and write `tfrecords` files, we need to use `tf.Example` protocol messages. Please note that every little piece of information contained in the data has to be stored through the use of `Etf.Example`. Furthermore, to write the information to disk, `tf.io.TFRecordWriter` is used. To read back the information from the disk, you can use `tf.io.TFRecordReader`.

TensorFlow protocol messages – tf.Example

`tf.Example` is a {`'string':tf.train.Feature`} mapping (Python dictionaries), where `'string'` could be any name; for example, `'image'`, `'features'`, or `'label'`.

`tf.train.Feature` can be one of the following three types:

- `tf.train.BytesList`: This is used for `string` or `byte` information
- `tf.train.FloatList`: This is used for `float` or `double` information
- `tf.train.Int64List`: This is used for `bool`, `enum`, and all kinds of integers, such as `int32`, `uint32`, `int64`, `uint64`, and so on

`tf.Example` messages can be serialized, written, and read into `tfrecords` files by converting standard TensorFlow types using the following shortcut functions:

The functions in the following code block can be used to convert a value into a type that's compatible with `tf.Example`. Please refer to `https://www.tensorflow.org/alpha/tutorials/load_data/tf_records` for more information.

```
def _bytes_feature(value):
  """Returns a bytes_list from a string / byte."""
  if isinstance(value, type(tf.constant(0))):
    value = value.numpy() # BytesList won't unpack a string from an
EagerTensor.
  return tf.train.Feature(bytes_list=tf.train.BytesList(value=[value]))

def _float_feature(value):
```

```
  """Returns a float_list from a float / double."""
  return tf.train.Feature(float_list=tf.train.FloatList(value=[value]))

def _int64_feature(value):
  """Returns an int64_list from a bool / enum / int / uint."""
  return tf.train.Feature(int64_list=tf.train.Int64List(value=[value]))

print(_bytes_feature(b'test_string'))
print(_bytes_feature(u'test_bytes'.encode('utf-8')))
```

Let's look at some examples of how to create `TFRecords` files using images (PNG) and the `pickle` file format:

1. **TFRecords creation from images**: Let's assume that there is training, validation, and test PNG format image data in separate files in three folders named `train`, `validate`, and `test`, respectively. The number of images in each of the folders could be tens of thousands or much more for training data in the `train` folder. Our goal is to create `tfrecords` files for these images in an output folder with three subfolders, namely `train`, `validate`, and `test`. Also, as we explained earlier, we will create multiple `tfrecords` files, where we will have 1,000 image files to a single `tfrecord` file. We are doing this so that the size of the `tfrecord` file doesn't go over 100 to 150 MB. We will call this number `num_shards`. It consists of the following phases:

   - **Input data**: The example dataset, which is available at `https://github.com/PacktPublishing/What-s-New-in-TensorFlow-2.0/tree/master/Chapter03/images/input_folder`, has three subfolders: `train`, `validate`, and `test`. Each of them have a bunch of images, as listed here:

     ```
     input_folder/train/*.png, input_folder/validate/*.png,
     input_folder/test/*.png
     ```

   - **Output TFRecords files**: Our goal is to convert `TFRecords` files for each input data folder into the respective folders, as shown here:

     ```
     output_folder/train/*.tfrecords,
     output_folder/validate/*.tfrecords,
     output_folder/test/*.tfrecords
     ```

     Refer to the full code file in the GitHub repository of this book for more information: `https://github.com/PacktPublishing/What-s-New-in-TensorFlow-2.0/blob/master/Chapter03/images/create_tfrecords_from_images.py`.

The following code block is an excerpt from the code in the file found at the preceding link, which converts the input image file into a tfrecords file:

```
def _read_image_file(self, filename):
    # Read the image file.
    with tf.gfile.GFile(filename, 'rb') as f:
      image = f.read()
    d_file = os.path.basename(filename)
    if 'NHS' in d_file:
      label = 0
    elif 'HS' in d_file:
      label = 1
    return image, label

def _convert_shard_data_to_tfrecord(self, input_files,
output_file):
    """ Convert sharded input files to tfrecords
    """
    print('Generating %s' % output_file)
    with tf.io.TFRecordWriter(output_file) as record_writer:
      for input_file in input_files:
        data, label = self._read_image_file(input_file)
        example = tf.train.Example(features=tf.train.Features(
            feature={
                'image':
self._bytes_feature(tf.compat.as_bytes(data)),
                'label': self._int64_feature(label)
            }))
        record_writer.write(example.SerializeToString())
```

2. **TFRecords creation from custom files:** We will use the CIFAR10 dataset to create tfrecords from custom files. You can download this data from the following link: https://www.cs.toronto.edu/~kriz/cifar.html. More details are provided in the README file, which is available at https://github.com/PacktPublishing/What-s-New-in-TensorFlow-2.0/blob/master/Chapter03/cifar10/README.md. Please note that this CIFAR10 data contains 50,000 images for training the network, out of which we choose 40,000 as training and 10,000 as validation data. It has a separate 10,000 images for testing the model.

The following is some sample code for reading the pickle files and converting them into tfrecord files:

```
def read_pickle_from_file(filename):
  with tf.gfile.Open(filename, 'rb') as f:
    if sys.version_info >= (3, 0):
      data_dict = pickle.load(f, encoding='bytes')
```

```
        else:
            data_dict = pickle.load(f)
    return data_dict

def convert_to_tfrecord(input_files, output_file):
    """Converts a file to TFRecords."""
    print('Generating %s' % output_file)
    with tf.io.TFRecordWriter(output_file) as record_writer:
        for input_file in input_files:
            data_dict = read_pickle_from_file(input_file)
            data = data_dict[b'data']
            labels = data_dict[b'labels']
            num_entries_in_batch = len(labels)
            for i in range(num_entries_in_batch):
                example = tf.train.Example(features=tf.train.Features(
                    feature={
                        'image': _bytes_feature(data[i].tobytes()),
                        'label': _int64_feature(labels[i])
                    }))
                record_writer.write(example.SerializeToString())
```

tf.data dataset object creation

As we mentioned earlier, the `tf.data` set of APIs provide the tools for building complex and efficient input data pipelines from raw data. As an example, the input pipeline can be built from image files from a distributed filesystem. It can be also built from raw text data if you're using a **natural language processing** (**NLP**) module. The following diagram shows the flow of `tf.dataset` object creation:

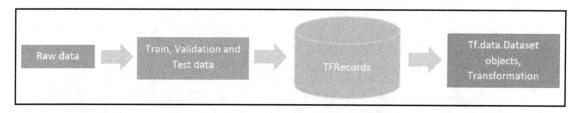

`tf.data.Dataset` is the primary class in the `tf.data` set of APIs and represents a sequence of elements, where each element contains one or more tensor objects. There are four main types of datasets, as shown in the following diagram:

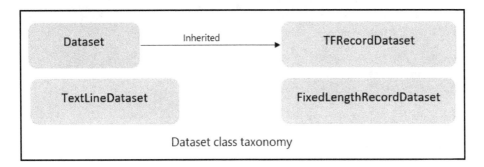

Dataset class taxonomy

 Throughout this chapter, all four types of datasets will be referred to as datasets and/or `tf.data.Dataset` for the sake of simplicity. Explicit types will be referred to when needed.

Definition-wise, `tf.data.Dataset` is a sequence of elements of one or more tensor objects, called components; each element in a dataset has the same structure. To inspect the type and shape of a dataset, developers can use two Python APIs, `tf.data.Dataset.output_types` and `tf.data.Dataset.output_shapes`, as shown in the following code block:

```
# Check type and shape of Dataset

dataset = tf.data.Dataset.from_tensor_slices(...)
print(dataset.output_types)
print(dataset.output_shapes)
```

The preceding code is an example of building an image data pipeline. The elements of the dataset could be a single piece of training data consisting of a pair of image and label Tensors.

In TF 2.0, dataset objects are Python `iterables`, which is a key difference from TF 1.x versions, where it needed `tf.data.Iterator` to iterate over dataset objects. The following code shows the difference between iterating dataset objects in TF 1.x and TF 2.0:

```
# The following code shows difference in iterating Dataset objects
# in TensorFlow 1.x and TensorFlow 2.0

dataset = tf.data.Dataset.from_tensor_slices(...)
dataset = dataset.shuffle(...)
dataset = dataset.map(...)
dataset = dataset.batch(...)

# TensorFlow 1.x (using one shot iterator, get_next)
```

```
iterator = dataset.make_one_shot_iterator()
next_element = iterator.get_next()

with tf.Session() as sess:
    for _ in range(...):
    element = sess.run(next_element)
    ...
# TensorFlow 2.0 (extremely simple where Datasets are Python iterables)

for element in dataset:
    ...
```

As you can see in the preceding code block, iterating through dataset objects is extremely simple now.

Creating dataset objects

Dataset objects can be created using two primary methods:

- Creation from source:
  - From in-memory numpy/tensorflow objects
  - From disk using TFRecords
- Applying a transformation to existing datasets:
  - Constructing a dataset from one or more datasets. This will be explained in more detail in the *Dataset transformation* section.

Since it's recommended to use TFRecords to create a tf.data.Dataset, let's see how that works. Then, we will cover ways to create datasets from other types of input.

Creating datasets using TFRecords

Once some TFRecords have been created, we can directly use tf.data.Dataset APIs to read them. The following is a block diagram of dataset creation using TFRecords:

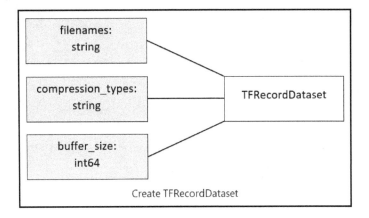

Create TFRecordDataset

You can use the following code to read `tfrecords` files from the dataset:

```
# You can read tfrecord files as below
dataset = tf.data.TFRecordDataset(tfrecords_file_names)
```

Creating datasets using in-memory objects and tensors

The simplest way to create `tf.data.Dataset` from in-memory objects is to use the `from_tensor_slices()` method, which slices arrays with respect to the first index in the data. We will refer to the `tf.data.Dataset.map()` API here, which is defined in detail in the *Dataset transformation* section. For now, `map(...)` simply means that a dataset is being modified (transformed) based on some function that is applied to every element of the dataset object.

There are two APIs that you can use to create datasets from in-memory tensors:

- `tf.data.Dataset.from_tensors()`
- `tf.data.Dataset.from_tensor_slices()`.

You can view the example code at `https://github.com/PacktPublishing/What-s-New-in-TensorFlow-2.0/blob/master/Chapter03/datasets/create_dataset_from_tensors.ipynb`.

Let's look at examples of these, as follows:

```
aa = np.array([1, 2, 3])
bb = np.array([2, 3, 4])
cc = np.array([3, 4, 5])
dd = np.array([4, 5, 6])

features = [aa, bb, cc, dd]
```

`from_tensors(...)` creates a dataset with a single element, comprising the given tensors. This is shown in the following code:

```
dataset1 = tf.data.Dataset.from_tensors((features, labels))
```

`from_tensor_slices(...)` creates a dataset whose elements are slices from the given tensor(s). When given a tensor with multiple dimensions, it constructs the dataset by slicing the first dimension of the tensor. An example of this is shown in the following code:

```
dataset2 = tf.data.Dataset.from_tensor_slices((features, labels))
```

Creating datasets using other formats directly without using TFRecords

As we mentioned previously, you can directly create a `tf.data.Dataset` using all the different file formats. We also explained the recommended way to create `TFRecords`. However, if you want to create datasets directly, without going through `TFRecords`, that is also possible. Here are some examples of creating a `tf.data.Dataset` directly from raw data:

- Using CSV files:

  You can use the `td.data.experimental.make_csv_dataset(...)` API to find the `.csv` file. You can define the columns that are available in the `.csv` file, along with `batch_size`, as follows. The complete code can be found at https://github.com/PacktPublishing/What-s-New-in-TensorFlow-2.0/blob/master/Chapter03/datasets/create_dataset_from_csv.ipynb:

  ```
  csv_file = "./curated_data/train.csv"
  csv_columns = ['square_ft', 'house_type', 'price']
  dataset = tf.data.experimental.make_csv_dataset(csv_file,
  column_names=csv_columns, batch_size=8)
  ```

If you need to select a few columns from the CSV file, you can do so by using `select_columns` arguments. For a more detailed overview, please refer to `tensorflow.org`.

- Using text data:

  The `tf.data.TextLineDataset(...)` API was designed to create a dataset from a text file. This is mainly useful for text data where each line consists of one data sample. Some examples include log messages, answers to questions, and so on. We will use the same example that we used in the previous section to show you how can we use text data to create a `tf.data.Dataset`. The complete code can be found at `https://github.com/PacktPublishing/What-s-New-in-TensorFlow-2.0/blob/master/Chapter03/datasets/create_dataset_from_text.ipynb`:

  ```
  def train_decode_line(row):    cols = tf.io.decode_csv(row,
  record_defaults=[[0.], ['house'], [0.]])    myfeatures =
  {'sq_footage':cols[0], 'type':cols[1]}    mylabel = cols[2] #price
    return myfeatures, mylabel

  def predict_decode_line(row):
    cols = tf.decode_csv(row, record_defaults=[[0.], ['house']])
    myfeatures = {'sq_footage':cols[0], 'type':cols[1]}
    return myfeatures

  line_dataset = tf.data.TextLineDataset('./curated_data/train.csv')

  train_dataset = line_dataset.map(train_decode_line)
  ```

- Using images:

  One of the most common input data pipelines is that of images, which can be either .jpeg or .png format. There could be potentially tens of thousands to millions of images in your dataset. We can't store all the images into memory due to hardware memory (CPU memory or GPU memory) limitations. `tf.data.Dataset` provides an efficient way to build this pipeline.

  In the following example, we have several `.jpeg`/`.jpg` files, all of which we will use to create `tf.data.Dataset`. You can find more details at `https://github.com/PacktPublishing/What-s-New-in-TensorFlow-2.0/blob/master/Chapter03/datasets/create_dataset_from_images.ipynb`:

  ```
  # Get images files
  file_pattern = ["./curated_data/images/*.jpeg",
  "./curated_data/images/*.jpg"]
  ```

```
image_files = tf.io.gfile.glob(file_pattern)
# Get labels
labels = []
for img_path in image_files:
  labels.append(get_label(img_path))

# preprocess images
def preprocess_image(img_path, label):
  img_data = tf.io.read_file(img_path)
  feat = tf.image.decode_jpeg(img_data, channels=3)
  feat = tf.image.convert_image_dtype(feat, tf.float32)
  return feat, label, img_path

# Create dataset of all image files
image_path_dataset =
tf.data.Dataset.from_tensor_slices((image_files, labels))

# Convert to image dataset
image_dataset = image_path_dataset.map(preprocess_image)
```

- Using multiple datasets:

  We can also create datasets from existing datasets by using the
  `tf.data.Dataset.map()`, `tf.data.Dataset.zip()`, and
  `tf.data.Dataset.concatenate()` APIs. These will be explained in the next
  section, where we will talk about transforming datasets.

Transforming datasets

Once the dataset objects have been created, they need to be transformed based on the
model's requirements. The following diagram shows the flow of dataset transformation:

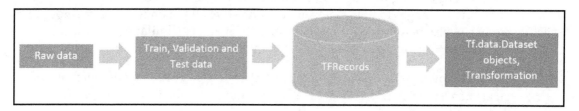

Some of the most important transformations are as follows:

- **Data rearrangements**: These might be needed to select a portion of data instead of taking the entire dataset. They can be useful for doing experiments with a subset of data.
- **Data cleanups**: These are extremely important. It could just be as simple as cleaning up a date format, such as from YYYY/MM/DD to MM-DD-YYYY, or removing data that has missing values or incorrect numbers. Other examples of data cleansing is removing stop words from text files for an NLP module.
- **Data standardization and normalization**: These are crucial for data where one or more features are coming from various sources and have different units and scales. Most linear regression and logistic regression algorithms assume that data has a Gaussian distribution. You might want to standardize one or more features of your data so that they have a mean equal to 0 and a standard deviation of 1. Data standardization is also needed where features of the data are coming from different sources at a different scale. Data normalization rescales features to a specific range (for example, between 0 and 1 or -1 and 1), which could be required for different activation functions, such as sigmoid, tanh, and so on.

 Please note that batch normalization techniques are used instead when building the model. This will be explained in `Chapter 4`, *Model Training and Use of TensorBoard* in detail.

- **Feature engineering**: This is another important part of model training. In some cases, features from your data could be very similar and correlated, such as the age of a person and their health index. As part of data transformation, engineers might want for creating new features from one or more other features that have the same patterns.
- **Training data augmentation**: This is another extremely important type of data transformation that you can use for creating more training data from a class or an imbalanced training dataset, to capture variations in the training data, or to simply add noise to the data to capture data distribution. An example would be to flip or rotate images and add some noise to them.

The following diagram gives a general idea of dataset transformation:

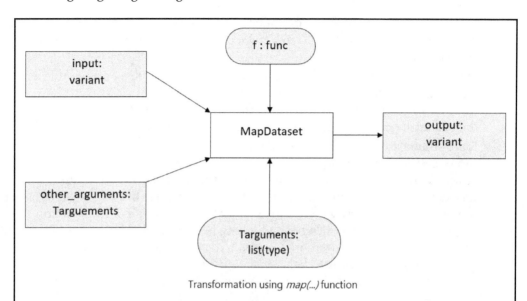

Transformation using *map(...)* function

Data transformation can be done either offline or online. In offline data transformation, an engineer does all the modifications and changes, and transforms the data directly either from raw data or while creating tfrecords before tf.data.Dataset object creation. This is a one-time process and doesn't increase the training runtime. Alternatively, engineers can do data transformation online by using tf.data.Dataset.map() and other related APIs after dataset object creation. This online transformation is done on the fly at training time and might increase the overall training runtime.

As a recommendation, you might want to transform data offline in case permanent changes are made to it that are required for your training flow; however, if you want to do several experiments with temporary changes to the data in place while you're training your models, online data transformation is recommended.

TF 2.0 provides a rich set of transformation APIs via the use of tf.data.Dataset.map() and other functions. We will go over these now.

The map function

This transformation API performs a `map_func` input on each element of the dataset. For those of you who have used pandas' `Dataframe.apply(...)`, `map(...)` is very similar to that. As an argument of the `map(...)` API, it takes a function that is applied to each element of the dataset. This function, in turn, takes a `tf.Tensor` object that represents a single element from the input dataset and returns a newly transformed `tf.Tensor` object. Please note that the order of elements in the output remains the same as it is for the input dataset:

```
ds = tf.data.Dataset.range(1, 6) # [1, 2, 3, 4, 5]
ds.map(lambda x: x + 1)
```

It's important to define the input signature of `map_func` correctly, as per the structure of each element in the dataset:

```
a = [1, 2, 3, 4, 5]
ds = tf.data.Dataset.from_tensor_slices(a)
result = a.map(lambda x: ...)

b = [(2, 1), (3, 5), (6, 6)]
ds = tf.data.Dataset.from_tensor_slices(b)
def map_func(input):
  output1 = input[0] + 1
  output2 = input[1] + 2
  return output1, output2

ds=ds.map(map_func)
```

The flat_map function

This transformation maps the `map_func` input across the input dataset and flattens the results. This is used to make sure that the order of your dataset remains the same. `map_func` must return a dataset here:

```
a = Dataset.from_tensor_slices([ [1, 2, 3], [4, 5, 6], [7, 8, 9] ])

a.flat_map(lambda x: Dataset.from_tensor_slices(x + 1)) # ==>
# [ 2, 3, 4, 5, 6, 7, 8, 9, 10 ]
```

The zip function

This API is similar to Python's built-in zip(...) function. The difference between Python's zip(...) function and the tf.data.Dataset.zip(...) function is that the latter can take in a nested structure of datasets:

```
a = Dataset.range(1, 4) # ==> [ 1, 2, 3 ]
b = Dataset.range(4, 7) # ==> [ 4, 5, 6 ]
c = Dataset.range(7, 13).batch(2) # ==> [ [7, 8], [9, 10], [11, 12] ]
d = Dataset.range(13, 15) # ==> [ 13, 14 ]

# The nested structure of the `datasets` argument determines the
# structure of elements in the resulting dataset.
Dataset.zip((a, b)) # ==> [ (1, 4), (2, 5), (3, 6) ]
Dataset.zip((b, a)) # ==> [ (4, 1), (5, 2), (6, 3) ]

# The `datasets` argument may contain an arbitrary number of
# datasets.
Dataset.zip((a, b, c)) # ==> [ (1, 4, [7, 8]),
                       #   (2, 5, [9, 10]),
                       #   (3, 6, [11, 12]) ]

# The number of elements in the resulting dataset is the same as
# the size of the smallest dataset in `datasets`.
Dataset.zip((a, d)) # ==> [ (1, 13), (2, 14) ]
```

The concatenate function

This transformation API creates a new dataset by concatenating the input dataset with this dataset:

```
a = tf.data.Dataset.range(1, 4) # ==> [ 1, 2, 3 ]
b = tf.data.Dataset.range(4, 8) # ==> [ 4, 5, 6, 7 ]
c = a.concatenate(b) # ==> [ 1, 2, 3, 4, 5, 6, 7 ]
```

The interleave function

This API transforms each element of the dataset using map_func and interleaves the results. For example, you can use Dataset.interleave() to process many input files concurrently:

```
# Preprocess 4 files concurrently, and interleave blocks of 16 records from
# each file.
filenames = ["/var/data/file1.txt", "/var/data/file2.txt", ...]
```

```
dataset = (Dataset.from_tensor_slices(filenames)
        .interleave(lambda x:
            TextLineDataset(x).map(parse_fn, num_parallel_calls=1),
            cycle_length=4, block_length=16))
```

The `cycle_length` and `block_length` arguments control the order in which elements are produced. `cycle_length` controls the number of input elements that are processed concurrently. If you set `cycle_length` to 1, for example, this transformation will handle one input element at a time and will produce identical results to `tf.data.Dataset.flat_map`. In general, this transformation will apply `map_func` to `cycle_length` input elements, open iterators on the returned dataset objects, and cycle through them, producing `block_length` consecutive elements from each iterator, before consuming the next input element each time it reaches the end of an iterator:

```
a = Dataset.range(1, 6) # ==> [ 1, 2, 3, 4, 5 ]

# NOTE: New lines indicate "block" boundaries.
a.interleave(lambda x: Dataset.from_tensors(x).repeat(6),
            cycle_length=2, block_length=4)
# ==> [1, 1, 1, 1,
# 2, 2, 2, 2,
# 1, 1,
# 2, 2,
# 3, 3, 3, 3,
# 4, 4, 4, 4,
# 3, 3,
# 4, 4,
# 5, 5, 5, 5,
# 5, 5]
```

The order of elements yielded by this transformation is deterministic, as long as `map_func` is a pure function. If `map_func` contains any stateful operations, the order in which that state is accessed is undefined.

The take(count) function

The `take(count)` function creates a new dataset with the most count elements from the current dataset. This can be typically used to reduce the size of the dataset for debugging or minimalistic purposes. Also, if the count is specified as −1, or if the count is greater than the size of the dataset, the new dataset will contain all the elements of the preceding dataset.

The filter(predicate) function

This API filters the current dataset based on a conditional predicate function:

```
ds = tf.data.Dataset.from_tensor_slices([1, 2, 3])
ds = ds.filter(lambda x: x > 3) # ==> [1, 2]
```

Shuffling and repeating the use of tf.data.Dataset

Machine learning models must have a reasonable representation of data from the overall distribution of the training, validation, and test steps. In general, the raw data could be stored in a specific order, such as being stored with respect to each class together, or data could be stored in a specific source together. The raw data must be shuffled to ensure that the training, validation, and test data is spread across the overall distribution of the data. Also, it is recommended that the data is shuffled after every epoch. The following diagram shows the flow of shuffling and repeating the use of `tf.data.Dataset`:

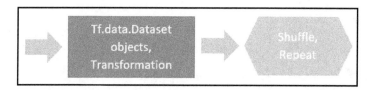

A good shuffle also helps reduce variance in data, which the model uses to help converge the model faster. It also improves generalization when it comes to testing and overfitting the training data. Due to these reasons, the training data needs to be shuffled. The `tf.data.Dataset.shuffle()` API provides an efficient way of shuffling on its own. It's extremely simple to use. Take a look at the following code:

```
dataset = tf.data.TFRecordsDataset(...)
dataset = dataset.shuffle(buffer_size, seed=None,
reshuffle_each_iteration=None)
```

The `shuffle(...)` API randomly shuffles elements of the dataset. The dataset fills a buffer with the specified `buffer_size` elements and then randomly samples elements from this buffer, replacing the selected elements with new elements.

 For perfect shuffling, a buffer size greater than or equal to the full size of the dataset is required.

For instance, if your dataset contains 10,000 elements but `buffer_size` is set to 1,000, then the shuffle will initially select a random element from only the first 1,000 elements in the buffer. Once an element has been selected, its space in the buffer is replaced by the next (that is, the 1,001-st) element, maintaining the 1,00-element buffer.

Once the dataset has been shuffled, we need to present data to the model repeatedly. To do so, we use the `dataset.repeat(...)` API. This just ensures that the model has a batch of shuffled data at all times within its pipeline:

```
dataset = tf.data.TFRecordsDataset(...)
dataset = dataset.shuffle(buffer_size, seed=None,
reshuffle_each_iteration=None)
dataset = dataset.repeat(count = None)
```

The `repeat(...)` API repeats the dataset count, which is specified as an argument.

Batching

Gradient descent combined with backpropagation is the most popular learning algorithm in recent machine learning or deep neural network systems. There are three kinds of gradient descent:

- Batch gradient descent, where all the data is presented to a model to learn from
- Mini-batch gradient descent, where a batch of data is presented to a model to learn from
- Stochastic gradient descent, where randomly sampled data is presented to train a model

Here, batch gradient descent is not practical in the majority of cases due to hardware memory limitations for large datasets. Also, stochastic gradient descent could be slow since a model learns from one piece of data at a time. Due to these reasons, mini-batch gradient descent is the most widely used algorithm. The following diagram shows the flow of batching:

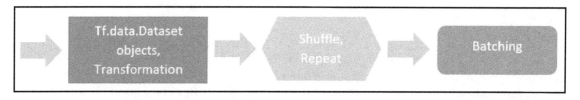

Furthermore, recent machine learning algorithms and deep neural networks are trained on GPUs, TPUs, and a massive number of CPUs in a distributed manner. Each of these GPUs or TPUs have their own in-memory limitations (for example, NVIDIA's 1080Ti GPU has 11 GB of memory available, whereas the Tesla V100 GPU has 16 GB of memory available). Since backpropagation-based gradient descent is used to train and learn ML model weights and biases, developers use mini-batch gradient descent; hence, it's important to have a good batch size so that the available GPU (or TPU) doesn't run out of memory.

`tf.data.Dataset` provides a great way to create batches of samples in an efficient and seamless manner, as shown in the following code block:

```
dataset = tf.data.TFRecordsDataset(...)
dataset = dataset.shuffle(buffer_size, seed=None,
reshuffle_each_iteration=None)
dataset = dataset.repeat(count = None)
dataset = dataset.batch(batch_size, drop_remainder=True)
```

The `batch(...)` API combines consecutive elements of this dataset into batches. `batch_size` is a hyperparameter that is passed to this API. In `Chapter 4`, *Model Training and Use of TensorBoard*, we will discuss and provide recommendations for batch size.

Prefetching

After batching is done, it's recommended to use the `prefetch(...)` API. This API transforms an input dataset into a new dataset that prefetches elements from the input dataset. This API is important because it collects the next batch that will be loaded into the input pipeline while the current batch is being served by the model:

```
dataset = tf.data.TFRecordsDataset(...)
dataset = dataset.shuffle(buffer_size, seed=None,
```

```
reshuffle_each_iteration=None)
dataset = dataset.repeat(count = None)
dataset = dataset.batch(batch_size, drop_remainder=True)
dataset = dataset.prefetch(buffer_size)
```

In general, the `buffer_size` argument that's specified for the `prefetch(...)` function should be as big as the `batch_size` argument specified for the `batch(...)` API in order to prefetch the next batch of data while the current one is being used to train the model.

Furthermore, if `prefetch(...)` is specified at the end of the pipeline, that is, after the `batch(...)` API is used, which is recommended, then `buffer_size` could be set to 1 or 2 as batching has already been done and `buffer_size` denotes one batch of samples.

For example, `dataset.prefetch(1)` will prefetch single elements (that is, a single data sample); however, `dataset.batch(128).prefetch(1)` will prefetch a single element of the batched dataset, which is one batch of 128 data samples.

Validating your data pipeline output before feeding it to the model

So far, we have learned about building the input data pipeline with several methods and techniques to extract and transform the data. As a recommendation, it's extremely useful to verify whether your input data pipeline is extracting and transforming the right data before it feeds it to a model. In TF 2.0, it is very simple to do this since dataset objects are Python iterables now. You can just iterate through the created dataset to the print values of the data, as follows:

```
ds = tf.data.Dataset.from_tensor_slices([1, 2, 3])
for data in ds:
    print(data)
```

Feeding the created dataset to the model

Once the dataset objects have been created, transformed, and shuffled, and batching has been done, it needs to be fed into a model (remember the L of ETL from the beginning of this chapter). This step has had a major change in TF 2.0.

One primary difference in input data pipeline creation in TF 2.0 is in its simplicity. TF 1.x needs an iterator to feed a dataset to a model. In order to do this, there are several iterators to iterate a batch of data. One is by using the `tf.data.Iterator` API from the dataset objects. There are one-shot, initializable, re-initializable, and feedable iterators in TF 1.x. While these iterators are very powerful, they add a good amount of complexity as well—both in terms of understanding and coding. Fortunately, TF 2.0 onward has simplified this to a great extent by making dataset objects Python-iterable.

Let's look at a comparison of TF 1.x and TF 2.0 regarding how they feed dataset objects:

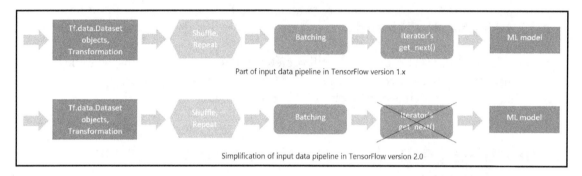

Part of input data pipeline in TensorFlow version 1.x

Simplification of input data pipeline in TensorFlow version 2.0

With TF 2.0, you don't need to worry about any iterators. If you are feeding to your non-`tf.keras` model, you can simply use a `for` loop since dataset objects are iterables now. If you are using the `tf.keras` model, you just need to pass a dataset to the `tf.keras` model. The following diagram shows the simplified pipeline for feeding data to the ML model:

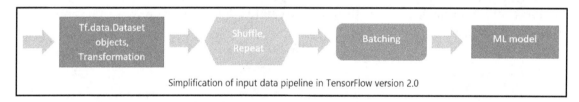

Simplification of input data pipeline in TensorFlow version 2.0

It's worth mentioning that, in TF 1.x, the `feed_dict(...)` and `queue runner` approaches are used primarily to feed data, which is not required in TF 2.0.

Now that we have learned how to build an input data pipeline, let's look at an example of complete end-to-end data pipeline by implementing what we have learned. We will use the CIFAR10 dataset to build a complete data pipeline, as well as building a classifier.

Examples of complete end-to-end data pipelines

So far, we have covered the creation of dataset objects and how to create batches of data to feed into a model. In this section, we will look at an example of an end-to-end input data pipeline and model training. We will build an image classifier using the CIFAR10 data.

In order to run the CIFAR10-based end-to-end example, you need to download the necessary data from https://www.cs.toronto.edu/~kriz/cifar.html. The dataset has been taken from a paper called *Learning Multiple Layers of Features from Tiny Images*, by Alex Krizhevsky, 2009 (https://www.cs.toronto.edu/~kriz/learning-features-2009-TR.pdf). This dataset contains the following information:

- 50,000 images with labels for training
- 10,000 images with labels for testing
- 10 class labels

After downloading and untarring the dataset, you will see a folder called cifar-10-batches-py, which will have the following files:

- batches.meta
- data_batch_2
- data_batch_4
- readme.html
- data_batch_1
- data_batch_3
- data_batch_5
- test_batch

The data_batch_* files contain the training data, whereas the test_batch file contains the test data. These files are in Python pickle format. In this end-to-end example, we will create tfrecords from the pickle files. The full code file is available in this book's GitHub repository, along with a README.md file, both of which can be found at https://github.com/PacktPublishing/What-s-New-in-TensorFlow-2.0/blob/master/Chapter03/cifar10/README.md.

Creating tfrecords using pickle files

For illustration purposes, we will use one of the `data_batch_*` files as validation data. We will use the rest for training. For example, if we choose `data_batch_4` as the validation data, then `data_batch_1`, `data_batch_2`, `data_batch_3`, and `data_batch_5` will be used as training data.

1. Let's create TFRecords using the CIFAR10 data:

```python
def create_tfrecords(cifar10_data_folder, validation_data_idx):
  """ function to generate tfrecords
  Creates three sub-folders, train, eval, test and put resp
  tfr files
  """
  batch_files = _get_file_names(validation_data_idx)
  tfrecords_outdir = './tfrecords'
  for data_type in ['train', 'eval', 'test']:
    input_files = [os.path.join(cifar10_data_folder, i) \
        for i in batch_files[data_type]]
    resp_dir = tfrecords_outdir + '/' + data_type
    shutil.rmtree(resp_dir, ignore_errors=True)
    os.makedirs(resp_dir)
    for ifile in input_files:
      batch_file_name = os.path.basename(ifile).split('.')[0]
      tfrecords_outfile_name = \
          os.path.join(tfrecords_outdir, data_type, batch_file_name
+ '.tfr')
      convert_to_tfrecord([ifile], tfrecords_outfile_name)
```

2. Use the created `tfrecords` method to create dataset objects:

```python
def create_datasets(self, is_train_or_eval_or_test='train'):
  """ function to create train sets
  """
  if is_train_or_eval_or_test is 'train':
    tfrecords_files = glob.glob(self.tfrecords_path + '/train/*')
  elif is_train_or_eval_or_test is 'eval':
    tfrecords_files = glob.glob(self.tfrecords_path + '/eval/*')
  elif is_train_or_eval_or_test is 'test':
    tfrecords_files = glob.glob(self.tfrecords_path + '/test/*')

  # Read dataset from tfrecords
  dataset = tf.data.TFRecordDataset(tfrecords_files)

  # Decode/parse
  dataset = dataset.map(self._parse_and_decode,
num_parallel_calls=self.batch_size)
```

```
    if is_train_or_eval_or_test is 'train':
      # For training dataset, do a shuffle and repeat
      dataset =
dataset.shuffle(10000).repeat().batch(self.batch_size)
    else:
      # Just create batches for eval and test
      dataset = dataset.batch(self.batch_size)
    dataset = dataset.prefetch(self.batch_size)
    return dataset
```

3. Feed the created dataset objects into a simple `tf.keras`-based model. Let's take a look at this model:

```
def build_model(self, learning_rate, dropout_rate, model_dir):
    """ build sequential
    Args:
      learning_rate (float): learning rate
      dropout_rate (float): dropout
      model_dir (str): path to store model
    """
    self.model = tf.keras.models.Sequential()
    input_shape = \
        (self.data.image_height, self.data.image_width, \
        self.data.image_num_channels)

    self.model.add(tf.keras.layers.Conv2D(filters=32,
      kernel_size=[3, 3], padding='same',
      activation='relu', input_shape=input_shape))

    self.model.add(tf.keras.layers.Conv2D(filters=32,
      kernel_size=[3, 3], padding='same',
      activation='relu'))

    self.model.add(tf.keras.layers.MaxPooling2D(pool_size=[2, 2]))
    self.model.add(tf.keras.layers.Dropout(0.25))

    self.model.add(tf.keras.layers.Conv2D(filters=64,
      kernel_size=[3, 3], padding='same',
      activation='relu'))

    self.model.add(tf.keras.layers.MaxPooling2D(pool_size=[2, 2]))
    self.model.add(tf.keras.layers.Dropout(0.25))
```

4. Then, flatten the dataset:

```
    self.model.add(tf.keras.layers.Flatten())

    self.model.add(tf.keras.layers.Dense(units=512,
```

```
activation='relu'))
    self.model.add(tf.keras.layers.Dropout(0.5))
    self.model.add(tf.keras.layers.Dense(units=10,
activation='softmax'))

    self.model.summary()

    self.model.compile(loss='categorical_crossentropy',
        optimizer=tf.keras.optimizers.Adam(learning_rate),
        metrics=['accuracy'])
```

5. Finally, feed in the dataset objects to train the model:

```
self.model.fit(self.data.train_dataset, epochs=num_epochs,
        steps_per_epoch=steps_per_epoch)
```

Best practices and the performance optimization of a data pipeline in TF 2.0

Here is a summary of the best practices to follow while building an efficient input data pipeline in TF 2.0:

- It's recommended to use a shuffling (shuffle) API before repeating the transformation.
- Use the prefetch transformation to overlap the work of a producer (fetching the next batch of data) and consumer (using the current batch of data for training). Also, it's extremely important to note that the prefetch transformation should be added to the end of your input pipeline after shuffling (shuffle), repeating (repeat), and batching (batch) the data pipeline. This should look something like this:

```
# buffer_size could be either 1 or 2 which represents 1 or 2
batches of data
dataset =
dataset.shuffle(count).repeat().batch(batch_size).prefetch(buffer_s
ize)
```

- It's strongly recommended to parallelize the map API by enabling the num_parallel_calls argument.
- For a dataset that's stored remotely, it's recommended to use the interleave(...) transformation to parallelize reading data from different files.

Built-in datasets in TF 2.0

TF 2.0 also provides a collection of datasets that are ready to be used with TensorFlow. It handles downloading, preparing the data, and even building `tf.data.Dataset` on its own, which can then be directly fed into the model.

Follow these steps to use these built-in datasets:

1. Install the TensorFlow datasets:

   ```
   pip3 install tensorflow-datasets
   ```

   Please note that `tensorflow-datasets` expects you to have a correct and complete installation of TF 2.0.

2. After `tensorflow-datasets` has been installed, you can view a list of available datasets by using the following code:

   ```
   import tensorflow_datasets as tfds
   tfds.list_builders()
   ```

   This will give the following output:

   ```
   ['abstract_reasoning', 'bair_robot_pushing_small', 'caltech101',
   'cats_vs_dogs', 'celeb_a', 'celeb_a_hq', 'chexpert', 'cifar10',
   'cifar100', 'cifar10_corrupted', 'cnn_dailymail', 'coco2014',
   'colorectal_histology', 'colorectal_histology_large', 'cycle_gan',
   'diabetic_retinopathy_detection', 'dsprites', 'dtd',
   'dummy_dataset_shared_generator', 'dummy_mnist', 'emnist',
   'fashion_mnist', 'flores', 'glue', 'groove', 'higgs',
   'horses_or_humans', 'image_label_folder', 'imagenet2012',
   'imagenet2012_corrupted', 'imdb_reviews', 'iris', 'kmnist', 'lm1b',
   'lsun', 'mnist', 'moving_mnist', 'multi_nli', 'nsynth', 'omniglot',
   'open_images_v4',
   'oxford_flowers102', 'oxford_iiit_pet', 'para_crawl',
   'quickdraw_bitmap', 'rock_paper_scissors', 'shapes3d', 'smallnorb',
   'squad', 'starcraft_video', 'sun397', 'svhn_cropped',
   'ted_hrlr_translate', 'ted_multi_translate', 'tf_flowers',
   'titanic', 'ucf101', 'voc2007', 'wikipedia', 'wmt15_translate',
   'wmt16_translate',
   'wmt17_translate', 'wmt18_translate', 'wmt19_translate',
   'wmt_translate', 'xnli']
   ```

Now, let's try to load some `mnist` datasets using the `tensorflow-datasets` APIs and feed them to a simple `tf.keras` sequential model. This code is also available in this book's GitHub repository, along with a README file, which can be found at `https://github.com/PacktPublishing/What-s-New-in-TensorFlow-2.0/blob/master/Chapter03/mnist/README.md`.

3. Next, we will load the `mnist` dataset and split the train data into 90% and 10% for train and validation, respectively:

```
def load_mnist():
    """ load tensorflow mnist built-in dataset """
    # Split the training data to 90, and 10 %
    ds_train_s, ds_validate_s = tfds.Split.TRAIN.subsplit([9, 1])
    # Download and load three datasets directly
    tfds_train, tfds_validate, tfds_test = \
        tfds.load(name='mnist',
            split=[ds_train_s, ds_validate_s, tfds.Split.TEST],
as_supervised=True)
    return tfds_train, tfds_validate, tfds_test

mnist_train, mnist_validate, mnist_test = load_mnist()
```

4. Once the dataset has been loaded, we can build our input pipeline using the `map`, `shuffle`, and `batch` functions, like so:

```
train_data =
mnist_train.map(scale).shuffle(BUFFER_SIZE).batch(BATCH_SIZE).take(
5)
validation_data =
mnist_validate.map(scale).batch(BATCH_SIZE).take(5)
test_data = mnist_test.map(scale).batch(BATCH_SIZE).take(5)

STEPS_PER_EPOCH = 5

train_data = train_data.take(STEPS_PER_EPOCH)
validation_data = validation_data.take(STEPS_PER_EPOCH)
test_data = test_data.take(STEPS_PER_EPOCH)
```

5. Once the data pipeline has been created, we simply use `fit()` to train the model:

```
model.fit(train_data, validation_data=validation_data,
epochs=NUM_EPOCHS)
```

As you can see, it is quite simple to create an input data pipeline using `tensorflow-datasets`.

Summary

This chapter has shown an overall approach to designing and constructing an input data pipeline using TF 2.0 APIs in a simple and suggestive manner. It has provided the building blocks of the different components of the data pipeline and given details of the APIs that are required to build the pipeline. A comparison between TF 1.x APIs and TF 2.0 APIs has been provided.

The overall flow can be summarized in two major passes: raw data management and dataset manipulation. Raw data management deals with raw data; splitting data into train, validation, and test sets; and the creation of TFRecords. Typically, this is a one-time process, which can also include offline data transformation. Dataset manipulation is an online transformation process that creates dataset objects, applies transformations, shuffles the data, and then repeats this and creates batches of the data with prefetching; these are fed into the model later on.

It's always recommended to use an input data pipeline, no matter the training data size and life cycle of the model training/inference. Since dataset objects are Python iterables in version 2.0, it's really simple to feed them into your model.

In the next chapter, we will learn about model training and using TensorBoard.

Further reading

While this chapter has tried to capture the most recent information about how to build an input data pipeline, TensorFlow is a fast-changing platform. The developers are adding new features every day. There're also thousands of open source contributors from the community, and they are adding features rapidly. It's strongly recommended to refer to `https://www.tensorflow.org` as much as possible to learn about correct API usages and/or changes.

4
Model Training and Use of TensorBoard

This chapter details a machine learning training pipeline to build, train, and validate state-of-the-art machine learning models, including deep neural networks. It describes how to integrate input data pipelines, create `tf.keras`-based models, perform training in a distributed manner, and run validations to fine-tune model's hyperparameters. It also touches on various concepts on how to export and save TensorFlow models for deployment and inferencing. Model debugging and visualization are the key tools used to debug and improve model accuracy and performance. This chapter also outlines the usage of TensorBoard, changes to it in TF 2.0, and how to use TensorBoard for model debugging and profiling a model's speed and performance.

TensorFlow 1.x version has strong support for low- and mid-level APIs to build machine learning models. It also has Estimator APIs, including pre-made Estimators, such as `LinearClassifier` and `DNNRegressor`, along with custom-made estimators to serve as high-level TF APIs. The support for estimators in TF 1.x was to provide high-level APIs, which are simpler to build in comparison to low- and mid-level TF APIs. Starting from TensorFlow 2.0, one of the major changes is to adopt the Keras API standard as high-level APIs instead of Estimators. This makes perfect sense for the TensorFlow development team since Keras APIs are by far the largest adopted API set in the machine learning community, and the creator of Keras, Francois Chollet, who is also a great Artificial Intelligence (AI) researcher, is now part of the TensorFlow development team. Initial support for `tf.keras` has been there in TensorFlow 1.x version; however, a full and complete experience of `tf.keras` is available in the TF 2.0 version.

In this chapter, we will skim through `tf.keras` APIs including sequential, functional, and model subclassing types of APIs. You will learn how to feed the input data pipeline to the model pipeline using `tf.data.Dataset` with the possible classified structure of the feature columns to the model. We will also touch on how to define loss functions, the most common optimizers, TensorBoard-based data, model debugging, visualization and profiling, and so on. Starting with TensorFlow 2.0, `tf.keras` APIs are tightly integrated into the TensorFlow ecosystem, which includes improved support for `tf.data` and newly available distribution strategies for distributed training across a wide variety of GPUs and TPUs. `tf.keras` also has seamless support for exporting trained models that can be served and deployed using TensorFlow Serving and other techniques on mobile and embedded devices using TensorFlow Lite.

We will cover the following topics in this chapter:

- Comparing Keras and `tf.keras`
- Creating a model using `tf.keras` 2.0
- Model compilation and training
- Custom training logic
- Distributed training
- TensorBoard

Technical requirements

It's assumed that readers of this chapter and this book know the basics of machine learning, neural networks, and deep neural networks. Also, as a prerequisite, it's assumed that readers know TensorFlow 1.x APIs. Further, a basic understanding of convolutional, recurrent, and feedforward layers in deep neural networks is required too.

Comparing Keras and tf.keras

`tf.keras` is TensorFlow's implementation of the Keras API specification. This is a high-level API to build and train models, which includes first-class support for TensorFlow-specific functionality, such as eager execution, `tf.data` pipelines, and estimators. `tf.keras` makes TensorFlow easier to use without sacrificing flexibility and performance.

Keras (the original website that defines the Keras API standard) has been an open source project that got tremendous attention from ML engineers and data scientists due to its simplicity and strength. Initially, the default backend engine for Keras (remember, Keras is a set of APIs) was Theano; however, lately, it has changed, with TensorFlow now as its default backend engine. You can also set the default backend engine to MXNet, CNTK, and so on. Keras APIs are extremely user-friendly, modular, and composable. Also, it's easy to extend for your specific needs. TensorFlow adopted Keras API standards and since then, the development of `tf.keras` using TensorFlow core functions has been going full swing. Now, with the release of TF 2.0, the TF development team has brought tight and efficient support of `tf.keras` high-level APIs. Also, it's worth mentioning that Keras and `tf.keras` are two entirely different packages and, as part of TF 2.0, `tf.keras` should be used. In terms of versioning, in TensorFlow 2.0, there is still a discrepancy with the version number of TensorFlow and `tf.keras` and you can try viewing this using `tf.__version__` and `tf.keras.__version__`.

Comparing estimator and tf.keras

TensorFlow 1.x has been recommending for using `tf.estimator` APIs for its high-level API set, which has pre-made estimators available with built-in models, such as `LinearRegressor` and `DNNClassifier`. Also, for a more granular and customized model, TF 1.x has custom-made estimators. Starting from TF 2.0, it's recommended to use only the rich set of pre-made estimator APIs that are packaged with linear classifiers, DNN classifiers, combined DNN linear classifiers, and Gradient Boosted Trees. These models are production-ready and widely deployed to be used. For any custom models, a suggestion is to use `tf.keras` directly instead of `tf.estimator` APIs. Also, it's worth noting that, to have better synergy with `tf.keras`, the pre-made models available in estimators will be ported back to `tf.keras` in future versions of TensorFlow 2.x.

As a recommended flow to build your training pipeline, if you know your machine learning problem types, such as classification and regression problems, you can use the following flow:

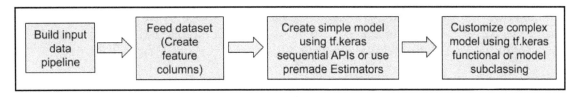

A quick review of machine learning taxonomy and TF support

Most of the learning problems can be solved using three primary kinds of machine learning techniques:

- Supervised learning to predict labels with the help of labeled data
- Unsupervised learning to group and cluster data that has no labels
- Reinforcement learning in which there is an environment through which an agent can learn to achieve the desired goal by taking action and getting feedback (rewards) from the environment

Generative and discriminative models can be used with all three of these kinds of machine learning techniques. A generative model tries to learn patterns and distributions empirically from a given dataset that has an unknown distribution and might use the learned model to generate new data as if it's coming from the same distribution. Some of the popular generative models are Gaussian mixture models, Hidden Markov model, Bayesian networks (such as Naive Bayes), and so on. An extremely popular generative model that came in 2014 is the generative adversarial model, which has attracted a lot of attention due to its strong success and potential. In addition to just learning a distribution, which can be used for unsupervised learning, generative models can also be used to do classification or prediction tasks (supervised learning), which use the conditional probability that a sample, x, belongs to a class, y, by calculating the probability $P(y \mid x)$ using the Naive Bayes theorem. Contrary to generative models, discriminative models are used to directly learn conditional probability, $P(y \mid x)$, for regression, classification, and other kinds of supervised learning problems. Deep neural networks can be used for building either generative or discriminative models.

TensorFlow provides rich sets of APIs to build the aforementioned generative and discriminative models. Further, in TF 2.0, there is an overall change in the philosophy of creating these models with the introduction of eager execution (explained in Chapter 2, *Keras Default Integration and Eager Execution*), which makes the use of `tf.keras` quite simple and easy to debug. Also, `tf.keras` APIs in TensorFlow 2.0 have enriched the overall power of what TF can do in the TF 1.x version. In this book, we mostly use `tf.keras` APIs to build, train, and predict neural network models and will not discuss low- or mid-level TF APIs unless mentioned otherwise.

TensorFlow's philosophy when building deep learning models and training them is to first define neural network layers (also known as building the computational graph consisting of nodes and edges); define a loss function, accuracy metric, and appropriate optimizer; and then train the model to update gradients. These three steps are reflected in tf.keras APIs using build, compile, and fit, as shown in the following diagram:

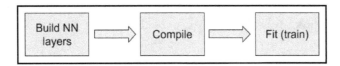

In the following section, we will first see how to build a model using tf.keras 2.0 APIs, which will detail the creation of computational graph nodes and edges. Then, we will cover compile and fit, covering the definition of loss and accuracy functions.

Creating models using tf.keras 2.0

In this section, we will learn three major types of tf.keras APIs to define neural network layers, namely the following:

- **Sequential APIs**: These are based on stacking NN layers, which could be either dense (feedforward), convolutional, or recurrent layers)
- **Functional APIs**: These help to build complex models
- **Model subclassing APIs**: These are fully customizable models; these APIs are flexible and require care to write

The following diagram shows a Python class hierarchy for these three APIs to build tf.keras.Model:

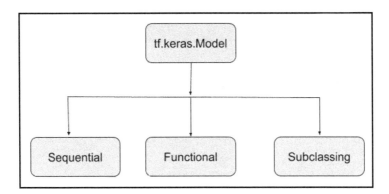

Let's create a relatively simple neural network to build a handwriting recognition classifier using MNIST data. We will use this example to demonstrate all three sets of APIs.

MNIST data contains 50,000 training datasets and 10,000 test datasets. These datasets have images of numerical digits and they are labeled to 10 classes (10 numerical digits). Each input image is of a size of 28 x 28 in grayscale. We will use a combination of convolutional layers and dense layers to build a supervised learning model to classify input images to one of the 10 classes. The preceding diagram gives us the details of the model we are going to build for this purpose.

We start building a network with the input layer of a size of 28 x 28 x 1 (please note that the channel length is 1 here since the MNIST images are grayscale images and they can be represented with either 0 or 1 values for every pixel, unlike RGB-based images, which need a channel length of 3).

The second layer is a convolutional layer of a 5 x 5 sized kernel and valid padding. Just for reference purposes, same padding means adding zeros to image boundaries so that output feature dimensions can be computed. Valid padding means we are ready to lose some information at the boundary of the image while doing convolution.

It's followed by another convolutional layer of a 5 x 5 sized kernel and then a 2 x 2 pooling layer. We add a dropout layer and then flatten the three-dimensional layer into a one-dimensional layer followed by a max pool layer. Using each of the three types of `tf.keras` APIs, we will build this model:

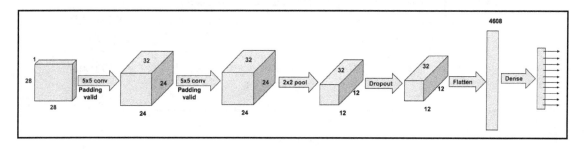

Sequential APIs

Sequential APIs are the simplest way to create a TF model and serve approximately 70-75% types of models. You need to create a `tf.keras.models.Sequential(...)` Python class and add desired layers to the model sequentially—this is also called the **stacking of layers**. These layers could be dense, convolutional, or even recurrent layers. You might need to provide the input shape of the first layer. The following are the steps to create a TF model using a sequential API:

1. Create a `Sequential` model class:

   ```
   model = tf.keras.models.Sequential()
   num_filters = 32
   kernel_size = (5, 5)
   pool_size = (2, 2)
   num_classes = 10
   ```

2. Build the model first by calling `build()` or `fit()` with some data, or specify an `input_shape` argument in the first layer(s) for an automatic build.

   Optionally, the first layer can receive an `input_shape` argument:

   ```
   model.add(tf.keras.layers.Conv2D(filters=num_filters,
       kernel_size=kernel_size,
       padding='valid', activation='relu',
       input_shape=input_shape))
   ```

3. Another `Conv2D` layer:

   ```
   model.add(tf.keras.layers.Conv2D(filters=num_filters,
       kernel_size=kernel_size,
       padding='same', activation='relu'))
   ```

4. Add a max pooling layer:

   ```
   model.add(tf.keras.layers.MaxPooling2D(pool_size=pool_size))
   ```

5. And add a `Dropout` layer:

   ```
   model.add(tf.keras.layers.Dropout(0.5))
   ```

6. Also, add a `Flatten` layer:

```
model.add(tf.keras.layers.Flatten())
```

7. Add a `softmax` layer with 10 output units:

```
model.add(tf.keras.layers.Dense(units=num_classes,
    activation='softmax'))
```

Please note the use of `tf.keras.layers` instead of `tf.layers`. TensorFlow 2.0 explicitly recommends using `tf.keras.layers`. With `tf.keras.layers`, you can specify weights, biases, initializers, and regularizers. With `tf.layers` and `tf.keras.layers`, there could be some differences in how the weight initialization is done and to get the exact API definition; it's recommended to look at `https://www.tensorflow.org/`, in the respective sections.

Functional APIs

Functional APIs build more advanced models than sequential APIs. For example, if you need a model with multiple inputs and multiple outputs, it's not possible using Sequential APIs. Functional APIs provide that flexibility. Also, using functional APIs, you can define models with shared layers. Further, models with residual connections can only be defined using Functional APIs.

The creation of neural network layers using Functional APIs happens through Python callables (Python objects that can be called). As part of building deep learning models, which are usually a stack of layers, and in contrast to Sequential APIs where you first create the `tf.keras.Sequential` model and then add layers one by one, in Functional APIs, we first create forward pass layer stacks—starting from input tensors to intermediate layers to output tensors using tensors and Python callable layers. Once the layer stack has been created, an object of the `tf.keras.Model` class is created by specifying input tensors and output tensors of the layer stack to the model.

We look at see Functional APIs now to build the same model as depicted in the diagram of the previous section:

1. Start with inputs, as follows:

```
inputs = tf.keras.Input(shape=(32,))
```

2. And then define various layers, as follows:

```
# first conv layer
conv1 = tf.keras.layers.Conv2D(filters=self.num_filters,
    kernel_size=self.kernel_size, padding='valid',
activation='relu')(inputs)
    # Another conv2d layer
conv2 = tf.keras.layers.Conv2D(filters=self.num_filters,
    kernel_size=self.kernel_size, padding='same',
activation='relu')(conv1)
```

3. Add a max pooling layer:

```
mp = tf.keras.layers.MaxPooling2D(pool_size=self.pool_size)(conv2)
```

4. And add a dropout:

```
do = tf.keras.layers.Dropout(0.5)(mp)
```

5. Flatten the layer:

```
ft = tf.keras.layers.Flatten()(do)
```

6. Add a `softmax` layer with 10 output units:

```
outputs = tf.keras.layers.Dense(self.num_classes,
activation='softmax')(ft)
```

7. And at the end, instantiate the `tf.keras` model with input and output:

```
model = tf.keras.Model(inputs=inputs,outputs=predictions)
```

Model subclassing APIs

Model subclassing APIs are used to build fully customized models by subclassing (deriving) a `tf.keras.Model` class object. This is achieved by creating layer stacks inside the constructor `__init__(...)` method of the derived class and they get set as an attribute to the class. Further, you implement the forward pass graph in the `call(...)` function.

Let's build model subclassing using the following class:

```
class MyModel(tf.keras.Model):

    def __init__(self):
        super(MyModel, self).__init__()
self.num_filters = 32
```

```
self.kernel_size = (5, 5)
self.pool_size = (2, 2)
self.num_classes = 10
self.my_input_shape = (28, 28, 1)
```

Let's define layers now:

```
# first conv layer
self.conv1_layer = tf.keras.layers.Conv2D(filters=self.num_filters,
    kernel_size=self.kernel_size, padding='valid', activation='relu',
    input_shape=self.my_input_shape)
# Another conv2d layer
self.conv2_layer = tf.keras.layers.Conv2D(filters=self.num_filters,
    kernel_size=self.kernel_size, padding='same', activation='relu')
```

Add a max pooling layer:

```
self.mp_layer =
tf.keras.layers.MaxPooling2D(pool_size=self.pool_size)
```

And add a dropout:

```
self.do_layer = tf.keras.layers.Dropout(0.5)
```

Flatten the layers:

```
self.ft_layer = tf.keras.layers.Flatten()
```

Add a softmax layer with 10 output units:

```
self.outputs_layer = tf.keras.layers.Dense(self.num_classes,
activation='softmax')
```

```
def call(self, inputs, training=False):
  conv1 = self.conv1_layer(inputs)
    conv2 = self.conv2_layer(conv1)
    mp = self.mp_layer(conv2)
    do = tf.keras.layers.Dropout(0.5)(mp)
    ft = tf.keras.layers.Flatten()(do)
    outputs = self.outputs_layer(ft)
    return outputs
```

After creating models using any of the APIs, it's always a good idea to use `model.summary()` and/or `tf.keras.utils.plot_model(...)` to review model details.

Model compilation and training

Neural networks model complex nonlinear functions, such as *sin(x)*, $x^{**}2$, and $x^{**}3$, to name a few simple ones and are made of a network (stack) of layers. These layers could be a mixture of convolutional, recurrent, or simply feedforward layers. Each layer is made up of neurons. A neuron has two ingredients to model nonlinearity—the weighted sum from previous layers followed by an activation function. The neural network tries to learn the distribution of given training data in an iterative manner. Once the neural network is built in terms of layers stack by specifying activation functions, an objective function (also known as the loss function) needs to be defined to improve model weights using an appropriate optimizer. There are multiple kinds of loss functions, such as the sum of squares loss used for regression problems and cross-entropy loss for classification problems, to name the most commonly used. Different kinds of learning problems may use customized loss functions as well. Using these loss functions, there are multiple optimizers on which can train the model, such as gradient descent, RMSProp, and Adam.

We saw how to build neural network layers or models in the previous section using either Sequential, Functional, or model subclassing APIs. The next step is to define the loss function and optimizer. The following sections explain the compile(...) API to show how the loss functions, optimizer, and accuracy metrics are defined using tf.keras APIs and the fit(...) API, which will demonstrate how model training is performed.

In Chapter 3, *Designing and Constructing Input Data Pipelines*, we discussed in detail how to create an input data pipeline using tf.data.Dataset and showed how easy it is to feed data to a model for training directly since datasets are Python iterables. We also saw, in Chapter 3, *Designing and Constructing Input Data Pipelines*, that batch size is specified while building the data pipeline. Batch size and learning rate are two of the most important hyperparameters while model training. The learning rate is specified with the optimizer function, which is an argument inside compile(...), and batch size is specified with the fit(...) function if you are not giving a dataset to feed the model. Remember that batch size is specified with the data pipeline.

The compile() API

The tf.keras.Model.compile(...) API helps to define the loss function and optimizers, as follows:

```
model.compile(optimizer='adam',
              loss='categorical_crossentropy',
              metrics=['accuracy'])
```

Loss can be defined simply using a string such as `mse` or `categorical_crossentropy`, or by specifying `tf.keras.losses.CategoricalCrossentropy`, as shown in the following code block. The same is true for the optimizer as well. However, in order to specify an explicit learning rate to the optimizer, you must use a Python optimizer class such as `tf.keras.optimizers.Adam`, as follows:

```
# Specify the training configuration (optimizer, loss, metrics)
model.compile(optimizer=tf.keras.optimizers.Adam(learning_rate=0.1),
              # Loss function to minimize
              loss=tf.keras.losses.CategoricalCrossentropy(),
              # List of metrics to monitor
              metrics=[tf.keras.metrics.Accuracy()])
```

The fit() API

`tf.keras.Model.fit(...)` is the primary API to train your model. It takes input training data and, optionally, batch size, callbacks, and so on, as its inputs:

```
model.fit(train_dataset, epochs=10,
      callbacks=[tensorboard_callback],
          validation_data=val_dataset)
```

Callbacks are hooks of specific utilities during model training. They are passed to the `fit(...)` function to customize and extend the model's behavior during training. There are many built-in callbacks that are useful—the following are some of them:

- `tf.keras.callbacks.ModelCheckpoint`: Saves checkpoints of your model at regular intervals
- `tf.keras.callbacks.LearningRateScheduler`: Dynamically changes the learning rate
- `tf.keras.callbacks.EarlyStopping`: Interrupts training when validation performance has stopped improving
- `tf.keras.callbacks.TensorBoard`: Monitors the model's behavior using TensorBoard

A typical use of callbacks is to create a list of callbacks and specify the `fit(...)` function as an argument:

```
callbacks = [
  # Interrupt training if `val_loss` stops improving for over 2 epochs
  tf.keras.callbacks.EarlyStopping(patience=2, monitor='val_loss'),
  # Invoke tensorboard
  tf.keras.callbacks.TensorBoard(log_dir=log_dir, histogram_freq=1),
```

```
]
model.fit(train_dataset, epochs=10, callbacks=callbacks,
        validation_data=val_dataset)
```

Saving and restoring a model

Monitoring training progress is extremely important and being able to review a model at every iteration or step of training is equally important to debug the model's performance. Further, once the training has been concluded, the model needs to be loaded for inference and deployment purposes. In order to be able to do this, the model's trained weights and parameters need to be saved for future use.

TF 2.0 provides support to do this easily as models can be saved during and after training. This gives the user flexibility to allow the restoration of training from a previous checkpoint and to avoid restarting the model's training completely to cut down a long training time. Further, these saved models can be shared between teams for further work. In this section, we will primarily discuss saving tf.keras.Models.

TF gives the flexibility to save model weights only or the entire model, including model weights, configuration, and optimizer details, and so on.

Saving checkpoints as the training progresses

Saving checkpoints can be simply achieved using tf.keras.callbacks, as follows:

```
# Create checkpoint callback
cp_callback = tf.keras.callbacks.ModelCheckpoint(checkpoint_path,
                                            save_weights_only=True,
                                            verbose=1)
model.fit(train_dataset, epochs=10, callbacks=[cp_callback],
        validation_data=val_dataset)
```

The preceding callback creates multiple TensorFlow checkpoint files, which are updated after each epoch training is done. Further, to use these checkpoints, recreate the model using exactly the same architecture as the original model for which the checkpoints were saved, build it, and load weights from any of the checkpoints using the tf.keras.Model.load_weight(...) API and use it for evaluation:

```
model.load_weights(checkpoint_path)
loss,acc = model.evaluate(test_images, test_labels)
print("Restored model, accuracy: {:5.2f}%".format(100*acc))
```

Manually saving and restoring weights

The model weights can also be saved in checkpoint files. This can be used to save trained weights for further training in the future:

```
# Save the weights
model.save_weights('./checkpoints/my_checkpoint')
# Restore the weights
model = create_model()
model.load_weights('./checkpoints/my_checkpoint')
loss,acc = model.evaluate(test_images, test_labels)
print("Restored model, accuracy: {:5.2f}%".format(100*acc))
```

Saving and restoring an entire model

TF can also save and restore an entire model including weights, variables, parameters, and the model's configuration. This gives the flexibility to load the entire model without having the original code with which the model was trained. The entire model can be stored either in an HDF5 file format or the upcoming TF internal format using `tf.keras.experimental.export_saved_model`. At this point, the latter is still experimental so we will not describe that yet:

```
model = create_model()
model.fit(train_images, train_labels, epochs=5)
```

Save the entire model to an HDF5 file:

```
model.save('my_model.h5')
```

Recreate the exact same model, including weights and optimizer:

```
new_model = keras.models.load_model('my_model.h5')
new_model.summary()
```

Custom training logic

As mentioned earlier, TF 2.0 brings about default eager execution, which means that legacy TF 1.x custom training logic implementations based on a graph-based code flow are now obsolete. To implement such custom training logic in TF 2.0 with regard to eager execution, tf.GradientTape can be used. The purpose of tf.GradientTape is to record operations for automatic differentiation or for computing the gradient of an operation or computation with respect to its input variables. This is done by using tf.GradientTape as a context manager. TensorFlow records all operations executed in the context of tf.GradientTape onto a tape, which is then, along with the gradients, associated with those operations to compute the gradient of the recorded operation using reverse mode differentiation.

For example, the gradient of a simple cube operation can be calculated as follows:

```
x = tf.constant(2.0)
with tf.GradientTape() as tape:
  tape.watch(x)
  y = x ** 3
dy_dx = tape.gradient(y, x) # 12.0
```

tf.GradientTape records all operations that involve watched tensors, such as x in the preceding example. All trainable variables that appear in the tf.GradientTape context are automatically watched and recorded on the tape. This functionality can be disabled by setting watch_accessed_variables to False so that only the variables that are specifically watched by the programmer will be recorded.

Higher-order derivatives can also be calculated using tf.GradientTape by stacking the context managers onto each other and computing the gradient with respect to the previous order derivative.

tf.GradientTape also allows for more custom training logic since it provides options to manipulate the gradient before using an optimizer. This provides an alternate, more involved, and powerful method of training deep learning models than built-in tf.keras.Model.fit. To do this, all forward pass operations get recorded on tape and, to compute the gradient of those operations, the tape is played backward and then discarded. An important thing to note here is that a particular tf.GradientTape model can only compute one gradient.

To first implement the simple training of a model with tf.GradientTape, call the forward pass on the input tensor inside the tf.GradientTape context manager and then compute the loss function. This ensures that all of the computations will be recorded on the gradient tape. Then, compute the gradients with regard to all of the trainable variables in the model. Once the gradients are computed, any desired gradient clipping, normalization, or transformation can be performed before passing them to the optimizer to apply them to the model variables. Take a look at the following example:

```python
NUM_EXAMPLES = 2000

input_x = tf.random.normal([NUM_EXAMPLES])
noise = tf.random.normal([NUM_EXAMPLES])
input_y = input_x * 5 + 2 + noise

def loss_fn(model, inputs, targets):
    error = model(inputs) - targets
    return tf.reduce_mean(tf.square(error))

def gradients(model, inputs, targets):
    with tf.GradientTape() as tape:
        loss_value = loss_fn(model, inputs, targets)
    return tape.gradient(loss_value, model.trainable_variables)

model = tf.keras.Sequential(tf.keras.layers.Dense(1))
optimizer = tf.keras.optimizers.Adam(learning_rate=0.01)
print("Initial loss: {:.3f}".format(loss_fn(model, input_x, input_y)))
for i in range(500):
    grads = gradients(model, input_x, input_y)
    optimizer.apply_gradients(zip(grads, model.trainable_variables))
    if i % 20 == 0:
        print("Loss at step {:03d}: {:.3f}".format(i, loss_fn(model, input_x, input_y)))
print("Final loss: {:.3f}".format(loss(model, input_x, input_y)))
print("W = {}, B = {}".format(*model.trainable_variables))
```

Another feature added in TF 2.0 is the tf.function decorator. When a function is annotated with tf.function, it still works like any other Python function but will be compiled into a graph, which provides benefits, such as faster execution and GPU and TPU acceleration, and it makes it easy to export to SavedModel.

Not all functions need to be annotated with tf.function, as any function called inside an annotated function will also run in graph mode. Such functions are faster for graphs with multiple smaller operations, but others, with more expensive operations, such as convolutions, will see less improvement.

The tf.function decorator can also graph Python control flow, such as if, while, for, break, continue, and return. Running these functions allows for faster evaluation and hardware acceleration.

tf.function can also be used inside tf.keras models and training loops. The tf.function decorator is typically used on the model's call method to provide graph mode evaluation. Another more common practice is to use tf.function for one loop of training, as it simply controls flow. This way, more of the computations of the training process can be brought inside TensorFlow and will benefit from optimized operations.

The following snippet is an example of tf.function in tf.keras:

```
class CustomModel(tf.keras.models.Model):

    @tf.function
    def call(self, input_data):
        if tf.reduce_mean(input_data) > 0:
            return input_data
        else:
            return input_data // 2
```

The following snippet is an example of tf.function in training:

```
compute_loss =
tf.keras.losses.SparseCategoricalCrossentropy(from_logits=True)

compute_accuracy = tf.keras.metrics.SparseCategoricalAccuracy()

def train_one_step(model, optimizer, x, y):
    with tf.GradientTape() as tape:
        logits = model(x)
        loss = compute_loss(y, logits)

    grads = tape.gradient(loss, model.trainable_variables)
    optimizer.apply_gradients(zip(grads, model.trainable_variables))

    compute_accuracy(y, logits)
    return loss

@tf.function
def train(model, optimizer):
```

```
    train_ds = mnist_dataset()
    step = 0
    loss = 0.0
    accuracy = 0.0
    for x, y in train_ds:
        step += 1
        loss = train_one_step(model, optimizer, x, y)
        if tf.equal(step % 10, 0):
            tf.print('Step', step, ': loss', loss, '; accuracy',
compute_accuracy.result())
    return step, loss, accuracy
```

TF 2.0 also provides a way to create custom gradients to override the default gradient calculation. This is done by using the `tf.custom_gradient` decorator. A common reason to use custom gradients is to provide a numerically stable gradient for a series of operations, and they can also be used to clip the norm of the gradients.

To use the `tf.custom_gradient` decorator, we must define a function that both returns the desired computation's result and returns the gradient of the computation. An example of this is the implementation of gradient clipping during backpropagation:

```
@tf.custom_gradient
def clip_gradient_by_norm(x, norm):
    y = tf.identity(x)
    def grad_fn(dresult):
        return [tf.clip_by_norm(dresult, norm), None]
    return y, grad_fn
```

As we can see in the preceding example, the function not only returns a copy of the input tensor but also a function that takes the default gradients as an argument and returns the clipped gradient.

The `tf.custom_gradient` decorator's primary use is to allow for fine-grained of over the gradients of a series of operations and can be used to create a more efficient and stable implementation of a sequence of operations.

More examples on how to use `tf.custom_gradient` can be found at `https://www.tensorflow.org/versions/r2.0/api_docs/python/tf/custom_gradient`.

Distributed training

One of the strengths of TF 2.0 is to be able to train and inference your model in a distributed manner on multiple GPUs and TPUs without writing a lot of code. This is simplified using the distribution strategy API, `tf.distribute.Strategy(...)`, which is readily available for use. *The fit() API* section, which explains `tf.keras.Model.fit(...)`, showed how this function was used to train a model. In this section, we will show how to train `tf.keras`-based models across multiple GPUs and TPUs using a distribution strategy. It's worth noting that `tf.distribute.Strategy(...)` is available with high-level APIs such as `tf.keras` and `tf.estimator`, along with having support for custom training loops as well or for any computation in general. Also, the distribution strategy described here is supported for eagerly executed programs, such as models written using TF 2.0 `tf.keras` or in the graph using `tf.function`.

`tf.distribute.Strategy(...)` is quite easy to use. It provides good performance and is simple to change across different strategies. There are multiple types of distribution strategies available and we will focus primarily on using it with `tf.keras` models. The following are two steps used with `tf.keras`:

1. Create the appropriate `tf.distribute.Strategy(...)` class instance
2. Encapsulate the `tf.keras` model creation (which could be either Sequential, Functional, or model subclassing) and model compilation, also known as `compile(...)`, within `tf.distribute.Strategy.scope(...)`

Let's look at an example:

```
# create mirror strategy
mirrored_strategy = tf.distribute.MirroredStrategy()
# encapsulate model creation and compilation within scope
with mirrored_strategy.scope():
  model = tf.keras.Sequential([tf.keras.layers.Dense(1, input_shape=(1,))])
  model.compile(loss='mse', optimizer='sgd')
```

`tf.distribute.MirroredStrategy(...)` is the distribution strategy to use on a machine with multiple GPUs. The `scope(...)` API tells the encapsulated code to run distributed. By doing this, the model creation inside this scope creates mirrored (copied) model variables and compilation within the scope, which ensures the model is trained using this strategy. Afterward, `fit(...)` can be used to train models like you would without the distribution strategy. Replicating model's training on available GPUs and aggregating gradients are taken care of by `MirroredStrategy`.

Further, if you want to limit the model to run on only some GPUs on a machine, you can specify it as follows:

```
mirrored_strategy = tf.distribute.MirroredStrategy()
```

There are multiple strategies available, and the most common ones are
`tf.distribute.MirroredStrategy(...)`,
`tf.distribute.experimental.MultiWorkerMirroredStrategy(...)`, and
`tf.distribute.experimental.TPUStrategy(...)`. As is evident from the name of the APIs, the last two still have experimental support and will be stable in the future.

TensorBoard

TensorBoard is one of the most important strengths of the TensorFlow platform and with TF 2.0, TensorBoard has gone to the next level. In machine learning, to improve your model weights, you often need to be able to measure them. TensorBoard is a tool for providing the measurements and visualizations needed during the machine learning workflow. It enables tracking experiment metrics such as loss and accuracy, visualizing the model graph, projecting embeddings to a lower dimensional space, and much more. In contrast to TF 1.x, TF 2.0 provides a very simple way to integrate and invoke TensorBoard using callbacks, which were explained in *The fit() API* section. Also, TensorBoard provides several tricks to measure and visualize your data and model graphs, and it has a what-if and profiling tool. It also extends itself to be able to debug.

Hooking up TensorBoard with callbacks and invocation

TensorBoard can be used in two primary ways in TF 2.0. One way is to use it as a callback when training a model using `tf.keras.Model.fit()`, and the other way is to use `tf.summary` for lower-level models using `tf.GradientTape`.

To use TensorBoard in Keras model training, we need to specify a TensorBoard callback, which takes `logdir` in as a parameter. Other parameters of the TensorBoard callback include `histogram_freq`, `write_graph`, `write_images`, and `update_freq`. `histogram_freq` allows the user to specify how often the activation and weight histograms should be computed and requires validation data to be specified. `write_graph` specifies whether the graph of the model is to be visualized in TensorBoard, and `write_image` specifies whether to visualize the model weights as images.

Once the TensorBoard callback is defined, specify it in the `tf.keras.Model.fit(...)` callbacks parameter, which takes a list of `tf.keras.callbacks` classes. Take a look at the following example:

```
model = create_model()
model.compile(optimizer='adam',
              loss='sparse_categorical_crossentropy',
              metrics=['accuracy'])
log_dir="logs/fit/" + datetime.datetime.now().strftime("%Y%m%d-%H%M%S")
tensorboard_callback = tf.keras.callbacks.TensorBoard(log_dir=log_dir,
histogram_freq=1)
model.fit(x=x_train, y=y_train, epochs=5, \
          validation_data=(x_test, y_test),
          callbacks=[tensorboard_callback])
```

To use TensorBoard when training with other methods, such as `tf.GradientTape`, we can use `tf.summary` to log the required information with the following steps:

1. Create stateful metrics that accumulate the values from training and can be logged at any point in the process:

```
train_loss = tf.keras.metrics.Mean('train_loss', dtype=tf.float32)
train_accuracy =
tf.keras.metrics.SparseCategoricalAccuracy('train_accuracy')
test_loss = tf.keras.metrics.Mean('test_loss', dtype=tf.float32)
test_accuracy =
tf.keras.metrics.SparseCategoricalAccuracy('test_accuracy')
```

2. Then, define the `train` and `test` functions as normal, computing the metrics and accumulating them by calling them:

```
def train_step(model, optimizer, x_train, y_train):
  with tf.GradientTape() as tape:
    predictions = model(x_train, training=True)
    loss = loss_object(y_train, predictions)
  grads = tape.gradient(loss, model.trainable_variables)
  optimizer.apply_gradients(zip(grads, model.trainable_variables))
  train_loss(loss)
  train_accuracy(y_train, predictions)
def test_step(model, x_test, y_test):
  predictions = model(x_test)
  loss = loss_object(y_test, predictions)
  test_loss(loss)
  test_accuracy(y_test, predictions)
model = create_model() # reset our model
EPOCHS = 5
```

3. Finally, in the training loop, we can log the metrics using `tf.summary.scalar()` on the metric's `result` method:

```
for epoch in range(EPOCHS):
  for (x_train, y_train) in train_dataset:
    train_step(model, optimizer, x_train, y_train)
  with train_summary_writer.as_default():
    tf.summary.scalar('loss', train_loss.result(), step=epoch)
    tf.summary.scalar('accuracy', train_accuracy.result(),
step=epoch)
  for (x_test, y_test) in test_dataset:
    test_step(model, x_test, y_test)
  with test_summary_writer.as_default():
    tf.summary.scalar('loss', test_loss.result(), step=epoch)
    tf.summary.scalar('accuracy', test_accuracy.result(),
step=epoch)
  template = 'Epoch {}, Loss: {}, Accuracy: {}, Test Loss: {}, Test
Accuracy: {}'
  print (template.format(epoch+1,
                         train_loss.result(),
                         train_accuracy.result()*100,
                         test_loss.result(),
                         test_accuracy.result()*100))
  # Reset metrics every epoch
  train_loss.reset_states()
  test_loss.reset_states()
  train_accuracy.reset_states()
  test_accuracy.reset_states()
```

Visualization of scalar, metrics, tensors, and image data

TensorBoard also provides functionality to visualize custom scalars and image data. This is in addition to the metric visualization described previously. Custom scalar logging can be used to log a dynamic learning rate. To do this, use the following steps:

1. Create a file writer using `tf.summary.create_file_writer()`:

```
logdir = "logs/scalars/" + datetime.now().strftime("%Y%m%d-%H%M%S")
file_writer = tf.summary.create_file_writer(logdir + "/metrics")
file_writer.set_as_default()
```

2. Then, define a custom learning rate function, which will then be passed to the Keras `LearningRateScheduler` callback and log the custom learning rate inside the function:

```
def lr_schedule(epoch):
    """
    Returns a custom learning rate that decreases as epochs progress.
    """
    learning_rate = 0.2
    if epoch > 10:
        learning_rate = 0.02
    if epoch > 20:
        learning_rate = 0.01
    if epoch > 50:
        learning_rate = 0.005
    tf.summary.scalar('learning rate', data=learning_rate,
step=epoch)
    return learning_rate
lr_callback = keras.callbacks.LearningRateScheduler(lr_schedule)
tensorboard_callback = keras.callbacks.TensorBoard(log_dir=logdir)
model = keras.models.Sequential([
    keras.layers.Dense(16, input_dim=1),
    keras.layers.Dense(1),
])
model.compile(
    loss='mse', # keras.losses.mean_squared_error
    optimizer=keras.optimizers.SGD(),
)
```

3. Finally, pass `LearningRateScheduler` to the `model.fit` callbacks along with the TensorBoard callback:

```
training_history = model.fit(
    x_train, # input
    y_train, # output
    batch_size=train_size,
    epochs=100,
    validation_data=(x_test, y_test),
    callbacks=[tensorboard_callback, lr_callback],
)
```

Generally speaking, to log a custom scalar we need to use `tf.summary.scalar()` with a file writer, which is responsible for writing data for the run to a specific directory and is implicitly used.

A file writer is also used when writing image data for visualization in TensorBoard. The TensorFlow Image Summary API can be used to easily log tensors and arbitrary images and view them in TensorBoard. This can be helpful to sample and examine the input data and to visualize model weights and generated images.

To visualize images, `tf.summary.image()` is used to log one or more images when called in the context of the file writer. This function takes a rank 4 tensor in the form of (batch, height, width, channels), so any images not in that format must be reshaped before logging them to TensorBoard. This API can also be used to log any kind of arbitrary image data, such as a Matplotlib figure, given that it is converted into a tensor.

The following code snippet is an example of how to log a single image to TensorBoard:

```
img = np.reshape(train_images[0], (-1, 28, 28, 1))
# Sets up a timestamped log directory.
logdir = "logs/train_data/" + datetime.now().strftime("%Y%m%d-%H%M%S")
# Creates a file writer for the log directory.
file_writer = tf.summary.create_file_writer(logdir)
# Using the file writer, log the reshaped image.
with file_writer.as_default():
  tf.summary.image("Training data", img, step=0)
```

Graph dashboard

TensorBoard's graph dashboard provides the capability to visualize and examine a TensorFlow model. We can use this to quickly view the conceptual graph of a model's structure to verify its design or view an op-level graph to understand how TensorFlow understands and executes a program. Examining an op-level graph can also give an insight into how to redesign a model for a more optimal runtime.

Viewing an op-level graph is very simple in TF 2.0 with the following steps:

1. Add the TensorBoard callback to `Model.fit` to ensure that graph data is logged in TensorBoard.
2. Once run, open up TensorBoard and navigate to the graph tab on the top bar to view the graph. By default, TensorBoard displays the op-level graph, which displays the graph bottom to top, with the data input at the bottom:

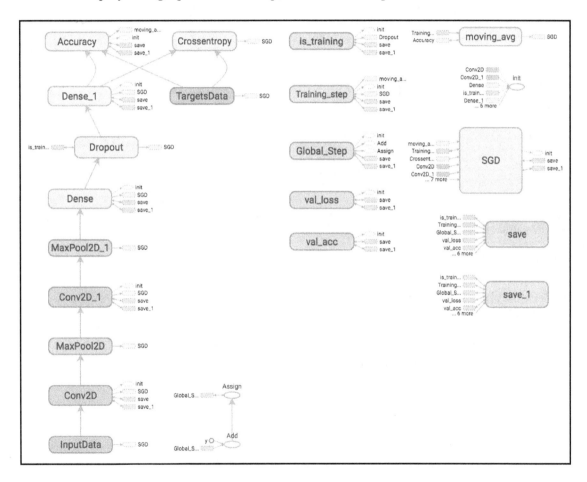

To navigate this dashboard, scroll to zoom, drag to pan, and double-click on nodes to expand them or see metadata.

As mentioned earlier, TensorBoard also displays a conceptual graph:

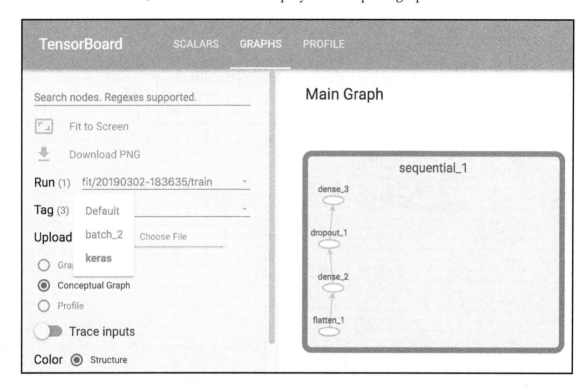

To see this, change the tag to **keras** on the left-hand side. It will display the model as a single node, and double-clicking this node displays the model structure.

Graphs of low-level operations and `tf.function` can be visualized using the `tf.summary.trace` API to log autographed functions for visualization on TensorBoard. To do this, use the following steps:

1. Define and annotate a function with `tf.function`:

    ```python
    # The function to be traced.
    @tf.function
    def my_func(x, y):
      # A simple hand-rolled layer.
      return tf.nn.relu(tf.matmul(x, y))
    ```

2. Use `tf.summary.trace_on()` immediately before the function call:

```
# Set up logging.
stamp = datetime.now().strftime("%Y%m%d-%H%M%S")
logdir = 'logs/func/%s' % stamp
writer = tf.summary.create_file_writer(logdir)
# Sample data for your function.
x = tf.random.uniform((3, 3))
y = tf.random.uniform((3, 3))
# Bracket the function call with
# tf.summary.trace_on() and tf.summary.trace_export().
tf.summary.trace_on(graph=True, profiler=True)
# Call only one tf.function when tracing.
z = my_func(x, y)
```

3. With a file writer context, call `tf.summary.trace_export()` to save the log data:

```
with writer.as_default():
    tf.summary.trace_export(
        name="my_func_trace",
        step=0,
        profiler_outdir=logdir)
```

Now, you can see the structure of the autographed function on TensorBoard.

Hyperparameter tuning

One of the most important parts of building a good deep learning model is choosing optimal hyperparameters for training the model itself. A hyperparameter is a parameter set by the engineer before model training. Some common hyperparameters include the dropout rate, learning rate, and type of optimizer used. The optimization of hyperparameters is a time-exhaustive process that involves training a model multiple times with different hyperparameters to find the optimal one, as there is no current insight on how to choose hyperparameters.

As such, TF 2.0 provides a tool to intelligently perform hyperparameter tuning, doing so by assisting in the process of identifying the best experiment to perform and the most promising hyperparameters to try.

To do this, use the following steps:

1. List the values you want to try for a specific hyperparameter and log the experiment configuration to TensorBoard. Then, adapt the TensorFlow model to include the hyperparameters in the model build. Once this is done, add the `hp.KerasCallback` callback to the `model.fit` function:

```python
def train_test_model(hparams):
  model = tf.keras.models.Sequential([
      tf.keras.layers.Flatten(),
      tf.keras.layers.Dense(hparams[HP_NUM_UNITS],
activation=tf.nn.relu),
      tf.keras.layers.Dropout(hparams[HP_DROPOUT]),
      tf.keras.layers.Dense(10, activation=tf.nn.softmax),
  ])
  model.compile(
      optimizer=hparams[HP_OPTIMIZER],
      loss='sparse_categorical_crossentropy',
      metrics=['accuracy'],
  )
model.fit(
      ...,
      callbacks=[
          tf.keras.callbacks.TensorBoard(logdir),  # log metrics
          hp.KerasCallback(logdir, hparams),  # log hparams
      ],
)
  _, accuracy = model.evaluate(x_test, y_test)
  return accuracy
```

2. Once the model is defined, the next step is to define an algorithm to cycle through all of the possible hyperparameters, such as grid search. This will cycle through all of the values of the discrete hyperparameters and the upper and lower bounds of the real value hyperparameters:

```python
session_num = 0
for num_units in HP_NUM_UNITS.domain.values:
  for dropout_rate in (HP_DROPOUT.domain.min_value,
HP_DROPOUT.domain.max_value):
    for optimizer in HP_OPTIMIZER.domain.values:
      hparams = {
          HP_NUM_UNITS: num_units,
          HP_DROPOUT: dropout_rate,
          HP_OPTIMIZER: optimizer,
      }
      run_name = "run-%d" % session_num
      print('--- Starting trial: %s' % run_name)
```

```
print({h.name: hparams[h] for h in hparams})
run('logs/hparam_tuning/' + run_name, hparams)
session_num += 1
```

For more complex hyperparameter tuning, a random search is more effective and efficient. This can be conducted by choosing each hyperparameter randomly and running the experiment, which can explore the hyperparameter space much faster than a grid search. Other more complex algorithms can be used as well.

3. Finally, the hyperparameter logs can be viewed by running TensorBoard on `logdir`, where the logs were written:

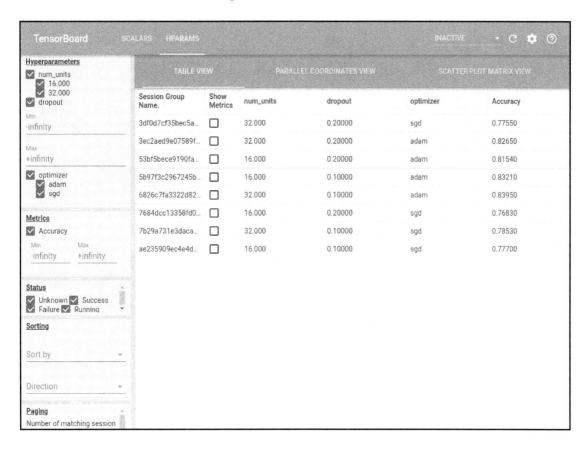

The left pane of the dashboard allows the user to filter logs by hyperparameters for ease of access and use. The hyperparameter dashboard has three views—**TABLE VIEW**, **PARALLEL COORDINATES VIEW**, and **SCATTER PLOT MATRIX VIEW**—each providing a different way to visualize the results. **TABLE VIEW** lists the runs and hyperparameters and displays the metrics. **PARALLEL COORDINATES VIEW** shows each run as a line going through an axis for each hyperparameter and metric and can be used to see which hyperparameter is more important. **SCATTER PLOT MATRIX VIEW** shows plots comparing each hyperparameter and metric and helps to identify correlations.

This tool provides easy tuning of hyperparameters and detailed logs and visualizations of the results in TensorBoard.

What-If Tool

TensorFlow 2.0 has introduced an extremely powerful tool viz **What-If Tool** (WIT), which helps with an easy-to-use interface inside the TensorBoard dashboard. However, you can use WIT only if the model has been served using TensorFlow Serving. TensorFlow Serving was explained in Chapter 5, *Model Inference Pipelines – Multi-platform Deployments*. Also, in order to use WIT, the inference dataset must be in TFRecords format.

Some of the functionality of WIT is the ability to compare multiple models with the same workflow, the visualization of inference results, similarity-based data arrangement, and the ability to perform a sensitivity analysis of the model by editing a data point.

Profiling tool

When using TensorBoard, which is available with TF 2.0, if you build and train your model using tf.keras APIs, there is already a **PROFILE** dashboard tab available, which can be used to see the various training times taken by your model:

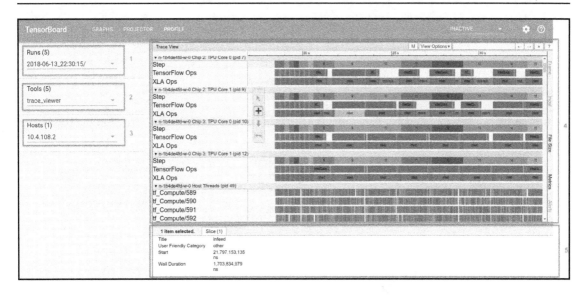

Summary

This chapter provided details on how to build a training pipeline using TF 2.0 `tf.keras` APIs and how to view build, compile, and fit a model using various available loss functions, optimizers, and hyperparameters in a distributed manner on GPUs using a distribution strategy. It also detailed out how to save, restore your model at training time for future training, and inference. With TensorBoard being one of the major strengths of TF 2.0, we provided details about how to efficiently use it to monitor training performance for loss and accuracy and to how debug and profile it.

In the next chapter, we will learn about model inference pipelines and deploy them on multi-platforms.

Questions

Should I use `tf.keras` **APIs or TF's low- and mid-level APIs?**

Check the chapter and try finding the answer to this.

When should I use `tf.keras` **Sequential and Functional APIs? Why do I need model subclassing?**

In general, for simpler models, `tf.keras` Sequential should be used. Most of models can be written using Sequential APIs. However, for those models that require multiple inputs and outputs and some specific connections, such as residual, Functional APIs should be used. For really customized models, you can use model subclassing.

Further reading

Users are encouraged to read `tensorflow.org` guides for transfer learning, which reuses pre-trained model weights and variables and transfer learning representations to another dataset, at `https://www.tensorflow.org/beta/tutorials/images/transfer_learning`.

Section 3: TensorFlow 2.0 - Model Inference and Deployment and AIY

3

This section of the book will focus on overall conceptual changes needed to migrate to TensorFlow 2.0 if you have used TensorFlow 1.x. It will also teach you about various AIY projects that you can do using TensorFlow. Finally, this section shows you how to use TensorFlow Lite with low-powered devices across multiple platforms.

This section contains the following chapters:

- Chapter 5, *Model Inference Pipelines – Multi-platform Deployments*
- Chapter 6, *AIY Projects and TensorFlow Lite*

5
Model Inference Pipelines - Multi-platform Deployments

What do you do after a model has been trained to perfection? Use it? If the answer is yes, then how do you use it? The answer you're looking for is **inference**. Simply put, the process of inference is what is needed to ensure that machine learning models can be used for serving the needs of actual users. Formally put, inference is the process of computing trained machine learning models efficiently to serve the user's needs. Inference can be performed on a variety of hardware types including servers, and end user devices such as phones and web browsers. As per user requirements, it can also be performed on different operating systems.

Previous chapters have focused on the process of how to build a model. This chapter will cover a detailed overview of the inference stage. First, you will cover a detailed overview of the practical machine learning workflow. Discussing important abstractions at a high level, you will have a detailed look into the `SavedModel` format and the underlying sub-concepts. You will also learn how to implement inference pipelines in different user-facing environments running on different software and hardware platforms. Further on, you will learn about the abstractions available in TensorFlow. This chapter also provides a detailed overview of how to use the abstractions discussed earlier along with other TensorFlow APIs to build pipelines to serve user needs in different computing environments, such as backend servers, web browsers, and edge devices.

The following topics will be covered in this chapter:

- Machine learning workflow – the inference phase
- Model artifacts – the `SavedModel` format
- Inference on backend servers
- Inference in the browser
- Inference on mobile and **Internet of Things (IoT)** devices

Technical requirements

In order to run the code excerpts given in this chapter, you will need the following hardware and software:

- **TensorFlow 2.0 (TF 2.0)** or higher (either of the CPU or GPU versions will suffice)
- Python 3.4+ (currently, the highest Python version supported by TensorFlow is 3.6)
- NumPy (if not automatically installed by TensorFlow)
- Docker (see `Chapter 1`, *Getting Started with TensorFlow 2.0,* for details on how to install Docker)
- curl (`https://curl.haxx.se/docs/install.html`)
- A Linux machine with a command-line interface

Each one of the Python code snippets in this chapter assumes that TF 2.0 is installed and has already been imported into the namespace. This means that, before executing any code block, please type in the following line first:

```
import tensorflow as tf
```

The code files for this chapter are available at `https://github.com/PacktPublishing/What-s-New-in-TensorFlow-2.0/tree/master/Chapter05`.

Machine learning workflow – the inference phase

One of the most common subsets of machine learning applications follow the *build once, use many times* paradigm. This type of application involves what is called the inference phase. In the inference phase, developers have to focus on running the model to serve user needs. Serving user needs might involve taking in input from the user and processing it to return the appropriate output. The following diagram describes a typical high-level machine learning application workflow:

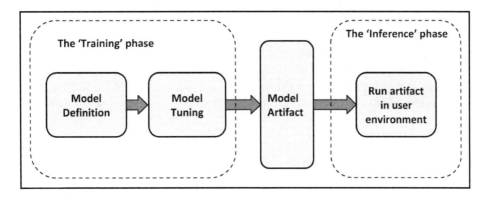

From the preceding diagram, we can see how the inference process fits into the overall picture. In applications that follow the *build once, use many times* paradigm, there are two distinct phases—training or model building, and inference. Both of these are coupled together via a shared model artifact. Depending on the specific use case, the details of the inference phase will vary based on the compute environment (both software and hardware) in which the model is intended to be run. In a typical real-world setting, pipelines are created for both the training and inference phases. At the completion of the training phase, the model consequently created is exported as an artifact. Construction of pipelines that do this were discussed in detail in Chapter 3, *Designing and Constructing Input Data Pipelines*, and Chapter 4, *Model Training and Use of TensorBoard*. Here, we will focus on exporting models and building various pipelines for the inference phase. The inference phase involves constructing pipelines that ingest this artifact and use it to compute outputs for user-specified inputs.

Understanding a model from an inference perspective

One thing that developers implementing machine learning-based applications can rely on to make life easy is that the process to serve models to users is more or less the same, regardless of the actual computations in the models being served. This implies that, if implemented correctly, engineers potentially wouldn't have to rebuild the deployment pipelines every time data scientists update the models. This can be achieved by leveraging the power of abstractions. A key abstraction here is the format in which models are stored and loaded. By introducing a standardized format, TF 2.0 makes it easy to train a model in one environment and then use it across platforms. In TF 2.0, the standard way to do this is through the SavedModel format. This standardized format is analogous to a build artifact in the software development pipeline. Readers can think of a model artifact as a snapshot that can be used to re-create a model without access to the actual code that created it.

Effectively, a model, at the time of inference, gets reduced to a black box with a set of predefined inputs and outputs and a uniform interface to interact with the underlying model. All a developer now needs to do is to build the infrastructure necessary to implement and execute this black box in a given environment. In the following sections, we will learn how to build pipelines to serve models across a variety of popular software and hardware environments.

Model artifact – the SavedModel format

The `SavedModel` format is the default model serialization and deserialization format used by TensorFlow. In layman's terms, this can be understood as a container that holds everything there is to reproduce a model from scratch elsewhere without access to the original code that created it. We can use `SavedModel` to transfer trained models from the training to the inference phase or even to transfer state between different parts of the training process. In a nutshell, it can be said that `SavedModel` contains a complete TensorFlow program along with model weights and descriptions of the various compute operations described. While working with the Python API of TF 2.0, it is now possible to export certain native Python operations along with the model. This is facilitated largely by the `tf.function` and `tf.autograph` APIs. In the following subsections, we will look at the `SavedModel` format in more detail and learn how to use it to export models and even write some code to build a model and export it.

Understanding the core dataflow model

Before we look at the nuances of the `SavedModel` format, it is important to possess a first-principles understanding of what a TensorFlow model actually is. For the uninitiated, TensorFlow implements the dataflow programming paradigm. Under this paradigm, programs are modeled as a directed graph of data *flowing* between different compute operations. This means that each node represents an operation (or computation) and edges represent the data. An incoming edge would represent an input to the node, while an outgoing edge would correspond to the output produced by the compute node. To illustrate this idea, let's look at the (rough) dataflow representation of the `tf.add()` operation. As we can see in the following diagram, the incoming edges correspond to the inputs of **x** and **y**. The outgoing edge, z (**x** + **y**), corresponds to the output of the node, which happens to be the sum of the inputs in this specific case:

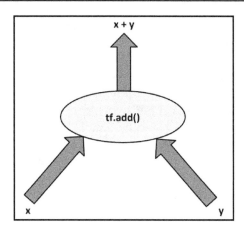

Using the dataflow paradigm allows TensorFlow to leverage a certain set of benefits when executing user code:

- **Parallelism**: Representing models as a directed graph lets TensorFlow identify which operations are dependent on each other and which ones aren't. This way, it becomes possible to execute independent operations in parallel, thereby speeding up the execution of the underlying compute graph.
- **Distributed execution**: A related benefit of parallelism is that the parallel execution can be either done on the same physical machine or a different one. TensorFlow also takes care of communication between these nodes.
- **Compilation**: TensorFlow's XLA compiler is designed to leverage the information in the dataflow graph to generate faster code through a series of optimizations.
- **Portability**: The dataflow graph is a language-independent representation of the code in your model. This makes it possible to build a dataflow graph in Python and restore it in a lower-level language such as C or Java for low-latency inference.

We have seen how a simple operation can be represented using the dataflow paradigm. A real-world TensorFlow program or model would be comprised of many such simple operations. This implies that the dataflow representation for such a program would be a composition of many such simple representations, with usually one or more nodes per operation. The `SavedModel` format can be understood as a serialization of this underlying dataflow graph. The role of higher-level APIs such as Keras and Estimators is interesting to mention here. Effectively, they abstract out the details of this dataflow graph from the users to the degree that users do not even have to think about it. They provide a set of high-level operations for the users to implement and then translate those into this dataflow graph that TensorFlow can execute. What this means is that, at the end of the day, any model created in TensorFlow, regardless of how it was created, translates into a uniform compute graph. This makes it possible to save and load all models using a single uniform format.

The tf.function API

As we have seen in Chapter 1, *Getting Started with TensorFlow 2.0*, and Chapter 2, *Keras Default Integration and Eager Execution*, eager execution enabled by default is one of the major changes introduced in TF 2.0. Chapter 1, *Getting Started with TensorFlow 2.0*, also briefly mentions that TF 2.0 is more closely coupled with the Python programming language. At the heart of this change is the low-level `tf.function` API. What this really does is blend the power of TensorFlow 1.x with the benefits of eager execution by enabling users to create TensorFlow graphs from Python functions. This is available for use, both as a callable function and a decorator. In this section, we shall briefly look at how it can be used in each one of these forms.

To illustrate how to use the `tf.function` API, let's consider a case where we try to create a simple TensorFlow graph to compute the sum of the sum and difference of two tensors. In short, we're implementing the following mathematical equation:

$$f(x, y) = (x + y) + (x - y)$$

To get started, let's first write a Python function that implements this functionality:

1. Create a function named `custom_function`, which accepts two variables, x and y. The function then returns the sum of the sum and difference of x and y:

```
def custom_function(x, y):
    _sum = tf.add(x, y)
    _diff = tf.subtract(x, y)

    return tf.add(_sum, _diff)
```

2. As you can see, the function we wrote is still a Python function. To verify this, type in the following line in your code:

    ```
    print(type(custom_function))
    ```

    You should see something like the following:

    ```
    <class 'function'>
    ```

3. We can use the `tf.function` API to turn this into a TensorFlow graph computation. This is very straightforward. It can be performed by simply passing the name of the Python function as an argument to `tf.function()`, as seen in the following snippet:

    ```
    custom_function_graph = tf.function(custom_function)
    ```

4. Let's now test our code. First, check the type of the output of `tf.function` using the following snippet:

    ```
    print(type(custom_function_graph))
    ```

    You should see something like the following:

    ```
    <class 'tensorflow.python.eager.def_function.Function'>
    ```

    As we can see in the preceding snippet, `tf.function` has successfully transformed a Python function into a TensorFlow graph computation. In many cases, this alone can result in significant efficiency gains.

5. Next, we test the logic of our code. Create two tensor quantities a and b and initialize them to `11` and `1`, respectively. Then, pass these to our newly created `custom_function_graph` instance. This is shown in the following snippet:

    ```
    a = tf.constant(11)
    b = tf.constant(1)

    print(custom_function_graph(a, b))
    ```

You should see the following output:

```
tf.Tensor(22, shape=(), dtype=int32)
```

As we can see in the preceding output, our code has produced a tensor with the value, `22`. This is same as the expected value of our custom function:

$$f(11,1) = (11 + 1) + (11 - 1) = 12 + 10 = 22$$

A more pythonic way to use tf.function in many cases would be to use it as a decorator. The following snippet presents an illustration of how to write the aforementioned code using a decorator:

```
@tf.function
def custom_function(x, y):
    _sum = tf.add(x, y)
    _diff = tf.subtract(x, y)

    return tf.add(_sum, _diff)

p = tf.constant(11)
q = tf.constant(1)
print(custom_function(p, q))
```

The tf.autograph function

So far, we've seen how to create TensorFlow graph code from Python functions. TF 2.0 takes the Python-TensorFlow coupling to a completely new level. The newly introduced AutoGraph (tf.autograph) function lets users write graph code using native Python syntax.

Currently, this feature only supports a limited subset of Python syntax. A detailed list of what syntax elements are currently supported is available at https://github.com/tensorflow/tensorflow/blob/master/tensorflow/python/autograph/LIMITATIONS.md.

A major advantage of this is that it enables developers to write intuitive Python code to achieve a certain task, which then automatically gets converted into highly performant TensorFlow Graph code. This means that developers can describe fundamental programming language constructs such as loops and conditionals in their intuitive Pythonic form, as opposed to the TensorFlow equivalents, with comparable performance.

In TF 2.0, AutoGraph is automatically invoked when tf.function is called. Users do not need to call it separately. The tf.autograph module contains low-level modules. Beginner or intermediate-level users are far less likely to have to use them directly and can safely ignore the details for now.

Let's look at examples to do this. Consider a function that computes the sum of all values in a given tensor. Let's implement it entirely using Pythonic syntax and then use `tf.function` to convert it into native TensorFlow compute graph code:

```
@tf.function
def sum_of_cubes(numbers):

    _sum = 0

    for number in numbers:
        _sum += number ** 3

    return _sum
```

To test the code we've written so far, let's create a tensor of integers between 1 and 5 (both inclusive). We then pass these to our function:

```
input_values = tf.constant([1, 2, 3, 4, 5])
result = sum_of_cubes(input_values)
print(type(result))
print(result)
```

This will result in the following output:

```
<class 'tensorflow.python.framework.ops.EagerTensor'>
tf.Tensor(225, shape=(), dtype=int32)
```

As we can see in the output extracted, the pure Python function we've written now gets transformed into a TensorFlow graph. This is evinced by the fact that the function now returns a tensor instead of a single number. The value of the output is the same as what is expected. Effectively, what we've demonstrated is that Python-specific syntax constructs such as a `for` loop and exponentiation operators were successfully translated into the TensorFlow graph code. This is the real power of `tf.function` and AutoGraph. As we've now effectively translated native Python code into a TensorFlow compute graph, it becomes possible to share this across environments using the `SavedModel` format.

Exporting your own SavedModel model

As we've seen in preceding sections, the SavedModel format is used to produce a reproducible representation of the current compute graph (the dataflow graph). This representation is independent of the specific code that was used to create the compute graph. It is also independent of the specific process used to construct this graph. For example, the SavedModel format doesn't actively distinguish between compute graphs created using native TensorFlow operations, Keras, or even tf.function. Though we interchangeably refer to this compute graph as a model, technically, it can also be considered a combination of a trained mathematical model and some additional code written around it for performing supporting tasks. In the TF 2.0 Python API, pre-built functionality for working with SavedModel is available in the tf.saved_model module.

In this section, we will look at how to create a compute graph the tf.function API. We will then store this in the SavedModel format and leverage it for performing inference tasks in different environments.

Using the tf.function API

As we've seen in earlier sections, the tf.function API enables us to write TensorFlow graphs and models using simple Python. Let's start things off by building a simple model that accepts a number or a list of numbers and returns the squares of the values in the list. We will then export the model thereby created into the SavedModel format. This is an important step for most of the following sections in this chapter. We will use this SavedModel artifact almost everywhere.

To get started, let's first write out a simple Python function that computes squares. We can then work our way backward from there:

```
def compute_square(number):
    return number ** 2
```

As we can see, the preceding Python method accepts a number as input and returns its square. Our end goal is to build a TensorFlow graph for performing this computation. Leveraging our learning from earlier sections, we know that one way to do this is by using `tf.function`. We choose to use the decorator form of `tf.function`. If you carefully observe the code snippet we've just written, you'll realize that we assume that the value passed to the `number` variable is a numerical value. This may not necessarily be the case in a real-world situation. To address this, we can specify what types of values can be accepted by this method in the decorator. This is done by fixing an input signature in the decorator. We fix this to be a one-dimensional tensor comprising 32-bit floats. Any inputs not meeting this criterion will automatically be discarded. Our modified code snippet, with error checking implemented now looks like this:

```
@tf.function(input_signature=[tf.TensorSpec(shape=None, dtype=tf.float32)])
def compute_square(number):
    return number ** 2
```

So far, we have managed to implement a TensorFlow compute graph that computes the squares for a given one-dimensional tensor. The only thing left to do now is to export this graph to disk in the `SavedModel` format. As you might recall, the API for working with `SavedModel` is available in the `tf.saved_model` module. On reading the documentation for this module (`https://www.tensorflow.org/versions/r2.0/api_docs/python/tf/saved_model`), we see that the `save` method might be helpful to us. One rough edge is that the `tf.saved_model.save` method only works with objects of the `Trackable` type while what we have is a `tf.function()` object (which is of the `Trackable` type or a subclass of it). To overcome this, we simply wrap up our code in a class that implements the `Trackable` interface:

```
class Square(tf.Module):

    @tf.function(
        input_signature=[
            tf.TensorSpec(shape=None, dtype=tf.float32)
        ]
    )
    def compute_square(self, number):
        return number ** 2
```

We now have our logic enclosed in a representation that is supported by the `save` method. Last, we create an object of the `Square` class (inherited from `Trackable`) and pass it to the `save` method:

```
sos = Square()
tf.saved_model.save(sos, './square/1')
```

You will now see that the model has successfully been exported to the `./square/1` directory. This can be verified by listing the contents of the preceding directory. Open the Terminal and type in the following:

```
cd <directory-containing-your-code>
ls -ax ./square/1
```

You will see something like this:

```
.    ..    assets    saved_model.pb    variables
```

In the upcoming section on analyzing `SavedModel` artifacts, we will look at what each one of these files contains and what role they play in the process of saving models.

Analyzing SavedModel artifacts

In this subsection, we shall have a detailed look at how `SavedModel` serializes and deserializes TensorFlow graphs. We shall also look at the `SavedModel` command-line interface, a powerful tool for analyzing the contents of `SavedModel` on disk and even running `SavedModel` locally!

The `SavedModel` format essentially describes a way to store a TensorFlow graph on disk. At a lower level, a part of what it does is codifies a format for representing this graph in files. As per this format, each graph is represented using a combination of constituent lower-level functions and their state. In TensorFlow parlance, these constituent functions identified with a name and are referred to as signatures or named signatures. These named signatures are further organized into groups called **MetaGraphs**. Most graphs typically have one MetaGraph but there are exceptions to this. State is represented using a combination of checkpoints and, optionally, files required to initialize certain nodes. These checkpoints are the same ones that are used to store state during the training stage. We discussed them earlier in `Chapter 4`, *Model Training and Use of TensorBoard*. The format discussed there remains consistent, regardless of the actual operations in the underlying model. To understand how this works in the real world, let's look at the contents of `SavedModel` on disk. Let's go back to the model we trained in an earlier section for computing the squares. When we list the contents of the model using the steps described in that section, we see the following:

```
.    ..    assets    saved_model.pb    variables
```

Of these, assets and variables are directories while `saved_model.pb` is a file. Their contents and role are discussed in the following:

- `saved_model.pb`: This file contains the constituent functions (or named signatures) representing the compute graph. This is an exhaustive set of all of the functions describing the underlying compute graph(s). As discussed earlier, these named signatures are organized in groups called **metagraphs**.
- `variables`: This contains a standard training checkpoint representing the state of the model at the time of saving. To verify this, you may list the contents of this sub directory. Type the following in a Terminal:

  ```
  cd <path-to-model-directory>
  ls -ax variables
  ```

- You should see something like the following:

  ```
  .   ..   variables.data-00000-of-00001   variables.index
  ```

- As you can see, this is very similar to what you might see for a training checkpoint.
- `assets`: This folder usually holds data used by the graph nodes. Examples of this include image files for performing comparisons and files with tabular data for holding pre-trained embeddings. Since our model doesn't rely on any such external information, this folder is empty for our model.

The SavedModel command-line interface

The `SavedModel` **command-line interface** (**CLI**) is a very handy tool that can be used to analyze various `SavedModel` instances and run them. It is very useful while debugging models on disk and can be used without reading, writing, or modifying any code. In this section, we shall briefly look at how to install this tool, use it to analyze the different components of the graph and run the compute graph.

 This tool comes bundled with TensorFlow binaries. If you've installed TensorFlow by building it from source, you'll have to install it separately. For installation instructions, please see https://www.tensorflow.org/beta/guide/saved_model#details_of_the_savedmodel_command_line_interface.

The two commands worth discussing briefly here are `show` and `run`. The former can be used to list the MetaGraph information whilst the latter can be used to execute the graph on a set of inputs via the command line. Detailed instructions can be obtained at each step by running the tool with the `-h` argument:

```
saved_model_cli -h
```

Instructions for specific commands can be obtained by calling the `-h` argument after the command's name. For example, if you would like detailed instructions about the `run` command, you'd type the following:

```
saved_model_cli run -h
```

To get a hands-on feel for this tool, let's go back to the model we built and trained in an earlier section on the `tf.function` API. As you might recall, the model accepts a tensor of numbers of any dimension and returns a tensor of the same shape containing the squares of the original elements. Let's first look at the number of metagraphs present in our model. To do so, type the following in a Terminal window:

```
saved_model_cli show --dir <path-to-model-dir>
```

For our model that computes squares, you should see the following:

```
The given SavedModel contains the following tag-sets:
serve
```

As discussed earlier, a metagraph is identified using tag-sets. Here, we can see that we only have one tag-set named `serve`. We might want to also look at the constituent functions making up this metagraph. To view the `SignatureDefs` (for details, refer to https://www. tensorflow.org/tfx/serving/signature_defs) making up this tag-set, you may type the following command:

```
saved_model_cli show \
    --dir <path-to-model-dir> \
    --tag_set serve
```

For our model that computes squares, you should see the following:

```
The given SavedModel MetaGraphDef contains SignatureDefs with the following
keys:
SignatureDef key: "__saved_model_init_op"
SignatureDef key: "serving_default"
```

Let's now see how we can use the `run` function to interact with this TensorFlow compute graph saved using `SavedModel` directly from the command line, without writing any code. As we can see in the output of the previous stage, there are two component functions. Of these, we choose to use the `serving_default` SignatureDef. We can now run it via the command line by providing the required inputs and obtaining the desired results. To do so, we need to pass a path to the model, the tagset(s), the input values, and the name of the component to run. For the purposes of this test, the tensor we would like to compute the square of is given by `[1, 2 , 3]`. The exact command is given as follows:

```
saved_model_cli run \
  --dir <path-to-model> \
  --tag_set serve \
  --input_exprs "number"="[1, 2, 3]" \
  --signature_def serving_default
```

The following is the output:

```
Result for output key output_0:
[1. 4. 9.]
```

From the output of the preceding stage, we can observe the following:

- The output tensor is of the same shape as the input tensor
- The values in the output tensor correspond to the squares of the values in our input tensor

Both these observations affirm that `SavedModel` is working correctly.

In subsequent sections, we will look at ways to serve this model in a variety of hardware and software environments.

Inference on backend servers

In today's world, distributed systems are everywhere. Ranging from the websites we browse to the apps that we use on our phones, hardly a day passes when we do not use distributed systems. Given this omnipresent nature, it is an obvious choice to adapt this paradigm for building machine learning systems. A typical pattern in building distributed systems is to perform resource-intensive (and data-sensitive) computations on backend servers whilst pushing lighter (and comparatively independent) compute tasks to the user's device. A large subset of machine learning applications falls into the resource-intensive category. Furthermore, machine learning models are built using data. In a significant fraction of real-world cases, the data used to do so is subject to privacy and security concerns. This further advances the case for implementing machine learning models on backend servers. In this scheme of things, the models are hosted and run on a fleet of backend servers controlled by the application builder. Users of the models send input data for these models to the servers, which then process the inputs, either individually or in batches, and return the results to the respective users. We have described the end-to-end workflow involved in building backend-powered machine learning applications in the following diagram:

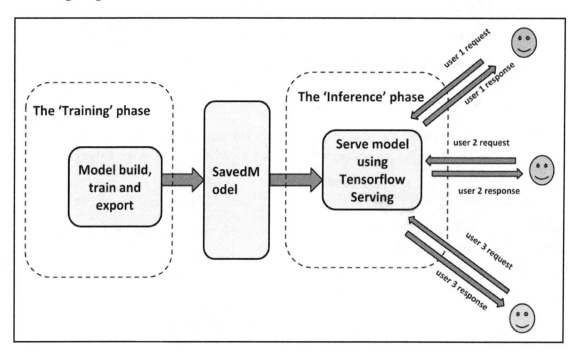

The workflow described in the preceding diagram illustrates the end-to-end pipeline of building a model from scratch and then serving it to users using backend servers. We see that the process is divided into two major phases: training and inference. In the training phase, the data scientists and other ML practitioners get together and build and train the model. Once the results are satisfactory, the model is exported. While a variety of formats are available for exporting the model, SavedModel is recommended over the others. In the inference phase, a fleet of servers consume the exported model. End users send inputs to these servers for processing and receive the results.

In this section, we shall look at different ways in which we can serve user requests by running models on servers. The primary tool in the TensorFlow ecosystem for doing this is TensorFlow Serving. TensorFlow.js is a good option for running models in the Node.js runtime environment. Other options include building custom serving solutions using the TensorFlow API for the respective programming language.

TensorFlow Serving

TensorFlow Serving is an integral part of the **TensorFlow Extended** (**TFX**) platform. As the name suggests, it is designed to be used for serving machine learning models. In a nutshell, it is a high-performance serving system designed for production environments. An important feature of TensorFlow Serving is that it exposes a consistent API to the downstream user, that is independent of the actual contents of the model being served. This makes it easy to experiment and re-deploy quickly without making any additional changes to the rest of the software stack. It ships with built-in support for TensorFlow models and can be extended to serve other types of models as well.

In this section, we will have a detailed look at TensorFlow Serving. Starting off with basic installation and setup, the following subsections describe how to set up a server to serve SavedModel through a series of hands-on examples. We will also briefly look at some of the key APIs made available by TensorFlow Serving.

Setting up TensorFlow Serving

Like most other components of the TensorFlow platform, TensorFlow Serving too can be installed in multiple ways. Using it via Docker images is the recommended approach here as it is relatively straightforward.

If container images don't work for you, a summary of other methods to install TensorFlow Serving is available at `https://www.tensorflow.org/tfx/serving/setup`.

Setting up TensorFlow Serving using Docker involves one simple step. This step though requires Docker to be installed on the host. For instructions on setting up Docker, please refer to `Chapter 1`, *Getting Started with TensorFlow 2.0*, or the *Technical requirements* section of this chapter. All you need to do is to pull the relevant Docker image for TensorFlow Serving to your host machine. To do so, type the following in a Terminal window:

```
docker pull tensorflow/serving:VERSION
```

The `:VERSION` part is to be used only when you would like to download a specific version of TensorFlow Serving. If omitted, the latest version will be downloaded by default.

Setting up and running an inference server

Now that we have TensorFlow Serving set up, let's use it to perform some real-world tasks. We can look at how to set up a backend server to serve the `SavedModel` format that we built in the preceding sections. We can use the Docker image downloaded in the preceding section to run this `SavedModel` format. To do so, we need to do two things:

- Bind the location containing the model on the localhost to a directory inside the container (`/models/<your-model_name>`)
- Bind the network port TensorFlow Serving is listening to a network port on the host

The general form of the command to do this is given as follows:

```
docker run -t --rm \
  -p <port-on-host>:8501 \
  -v <path-to-model-on-host>:/models/<model_name> \
  -e MODEL_NAME=<model_name> \
  tensorflow/serving&
```

The model server should now be running on your host at the port you've specified in `<port-on-host>`.

Let's now test our model by sending it some data for inference. We can interact with the model via the RESTful API. We should send an HTTP POST request with our input values to the server. To do so, type the following command in a Terminal window:

```
curl -X POST \
  http://localhost:<port-on-host>/v1/models/square:predict \
  -H 'Content-Type: application/json' \
  -d '{"instances": [1.0, 2.0, 3.0, 4.0]}'
```

You should see the following output:

```
{
    "predictions": [1.0, 4.0, 9.0, 16.0]
}
```

We have now seen how to use TensorFlow Serving to serve SavedModel on a backend server. This model is accessible via both gRPC and RESTful APIs. For details on these, please see the following links:

- https://www.tensorflow.org/tfx/serving/api_rest
- https://github.com/tensorflow/serving/blob/master/tensorflow_serving/apis/prediction_service.proto

Please keep in mind that each time you invoke docker run, a new Docker container is started on your host. This container might keep respawning and running in the background even after you've stopped interacting with it or even closed the Terminal window. This can lead to significant hidden memory consumption. A conscious effort is required to stop the container. To do so, perform the following steps:

Figure out the name or ID of the container that you've just started. Type the following into a Terminal window:

```
docker ps
```

As you can see in the output of the preceding command, each container has a name and ID. Either one of these can be used to uniquely identify the container. We need to use this to stop the container we've started. This can be done as follows:

```
docker stop <container-name>
```

You may also use the following:

```
docker stop <container-id>
```

You can now be assured that the container has been stopped and isn't consuming any of your computer's memory.

When TensorFlow.js meets Node.js

The introduction of TensorFlow.js has made it possible to run TensorFlow models in a JavaScript environment. As some of you might already know, Node.js is a cross-platform runtime environment that executes JavaScript code outside a browser. This makes it possible to use JavaScript code to write backend services. Integrating Node.js with TensorFlow.js makes it possible to serve machine learning services on backend servers from a JavaScript environment. Please see the documentation on how to go about this at `https://www.tensorflow.org/js/tutorials/setup`.

Inference in the browser

As you might recall, in an earlier section, we briefly discussed distributed systems. There, we discussed the scenario where the machine learning-based computation is primarily performed on host servers. Here, we will look at the scenario where these computations are performed on the user side, in the browser. Two significant advantages of doing this are as follows:

- Compute gets pushed to the user side. Hosts do not have to worry about managing servers for performing computations.
- Pushing models to the user side means that user data doesn't have to be sent to the host. This is a huge advantage for applications that work with sensitive or private user data. Inference in the browser hence becomes an excellent choice for privacy-critical machine learning applications:

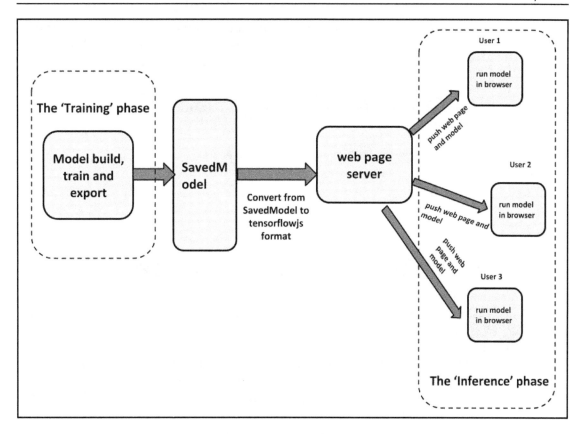

The workflow described in the preceding diagram illustrates the end-to-end pipeline of building a model from scratch and then enabling end users to run it within their web browsers. We see that the process is divided into two major phases: training and inference. In the training phase, the data scientists and other ML practitioners get together and build and train the model. This model is now exported in `SavedModel` format. However, TensorFlow.js doesn't directly support `SavedModel` formats yet. Hence, it becomes necessary to convert the model to a format supported by TensorFlow.js.

 For details on how to perform the conversion, please see `https://www. tensorflow.org/js/tutorials/conversion/import_saved_model`.

This converted model is now served to users through a web server, the same way as any other JavaScript code would be. Users provide the necessary inputs to the model. The TensorFlow.js model processes these inputs within the user's browser and returns the appropriate outputs.

Detailed resources for getting started with TensorFlow.js are available at the following links:

- `https://www.tensorflow.org/js/guide`
- `https://www.tensorflow.org/js/tutorials`
- `https://www.tensorflow.org/js/demos`

Inference on mobile and IoT devices

Smartphone use has grown exponentially over the last few years and continues to grow in an unabated fashion. Other IoT devices are also becoming increasingly commonplace in our day-to-day lives. These upward trends in usage adoption have interesting consequences for machine learning systems. These platforms are typically resource-constrained in comparison to normal host machines. As a result, additional optimizations are required to run inference on such devices. The TensorFlow platform supports building machine learning and deep learning-based applications that can run on different kinds of edge devices such as mobile phones and other IoT devices. The primary tool made available to this effect is the TensorFlow Lite platform. TensorFlow Lite can be used to build machine learning applications for a variety of platforms including Android, iOS, and even bare-metal microcontrollers! We provide a detailed overview of TensorFlow Lite in `Chapter 6`, *AIY Projects and TensorFlow Lite*.

The inference pipeline for TensorFlow Lite-based applications is somewhat similar to that for running inference in the browser. The first step involves building models using regular TensorFlow and exporting it to the `SavedModel` format. The model now might optionally need to be converted from the `SavedModel` format into a lightweight format that is consumable by the TensorFlow Lite Interpreter. This conversion is performed using the TensorFlow Lite converter (for details, see `https://www.tensorflow.org/lite/convert`). Post-conversion, the models are deployed to the respective edge devices using a channel specific to the platform in question.

Summary

In this chapter, we have taken a detailed look at the inference stage. Starting off by obtaining a basic understanding of what the end-to-end machine learning workflow looks like, we learned about the main steps involved in each stage. We also learned about the different abstractions that come into play while transferring models from the training phase to the inference phase. Taking a detailed look at the `SavedModel` format and the underlying dataflow model, we learned about the different options available to build and export models. We also learned about cool features such as `tf.function` and `tf.autograph`, which enable us to build TensorFlow graphs using native Python code. In the latter half of this chapter, we learned how to build inference pipelines for running TensorFlow models in different environments such as backend servers, web browsers, and even edge devices.

In the next chapter, we will learn more about AIY Projects and TensorFlow Lite.

AIY Projects and TensorFlow Lite

6

This chapter details how to deploy **TensorFlow 2.0** (**TF2.0**) trained models on low-powered embedded systems, such as edge devices, mobile systems (such as Android, iOS, and Raspberry Pi), Edge TPUs, and the NVIDIA Jetson Nano. This chapter also covers training and deploying models on do-it-yourself kits, such as Google **Artificial Intelligence Yourself** (**AIY**) kits. Other topics this chapter covers are how to convert trained **TensorFlow** (**TF**) models into **TensorFlow Lite** (**TFLite**) models, the key differences between them, and the advantages of the two.

This chapter is slightly different than the previous chapters, in the sense that it is simply an introduction to a wider concern of TF2.0; that is, the areas of hardware and applications. This chapter outlines some of the most popular systems that can be used to run TF models and perform deep learning tasks. Although each of these devices will be briefly explained in their respective sections, a quick Google search will offer much more detail for those interested.

The prior knowledge required to read and understand this chapter includes most, if not all, of the information detailed in the prior chapters, including data and training pipelines, `tf.keras` model creation, and model saving and checkpointing. You will learn about how to deploy TF2.0 trained models on low-power systems and on Google AIY kits. You will also learn about how TFLite functions and how to deploy and run it.

The following topics will be covered in this chapter:

- Introduction to TFLite
- Getting started with TFLite
- Running TFLite on mobile devices
- Running TFLite on low-power machines
- Comparing TFLite and TF
- AIY

Introduction to TFLite

TFLite is a set of tools to help developers run TF models on devices with small binary sizes and low latency. TFLite consists of two main components: the TFLite interpreter (`tf.lite.Interpreter`) and the TFLite converter (`tf.lite.TFLiteConverter`). The TFLite interpreter is what actually runs the TFLite model on low-power devices, such as mobile phones, embedded Linux devices, and microcontrollers. The TFLite converter, on the other hand, is run on powerful devices that can be used to train the TF model, and it converts the trained TF model into an efficient form for the interpreter.

TFLite is designed to make it easy to perform machine learning on devices without sending any data over a network connection. This improves latency (since there is no data transfer over networks), more privacy (as no data will ever leave the device), and offline capability (as an internet connection is not needed to send the data anywhere).

Some key features of TFLite include a tuned and optimized interpreter specific to the device (which supports a set of core operations optimized on devices with a small binary size), APIs for multiple languages (such as Swift, C, C++, Java, and Python), and pre-trained models and tutorials (which allow a novice to easily deploy machine learning models on low-power devices). TFLite is designed to be highly efficient and optimized, with hardware acceleration and pre-fused activations and biases.

The basic development workflow of TFLite is picking a model, converting it, deploying it to the desired device, and optimizing the model. The model can be anything, from a `tf.keras` custom-trained model to a pre-trained model taken from TF itself.

Getting started with TFLite

The first step of using TFLite is choosing a model to convert and use. This includes using pre-trained models, custom-trained models, or fine-tuned models. The TFLite team provides a set of pre-trained and pre-converted models that solve a variety of machine learning problems. These include image classification, object detection, smart reply, pose estimation, and segmentation. Using fine-tuned models or custom-trained models requires another step where they are converted into TFLite format.

TFLite is designed to execute models efficiently on devices, and some of this efficiency comes inherently from the special format used to store the models. TF models must be converted into this format before they can be used in TFLite. Converting models reduces file size and add optimizations that don't affect accuracy. Other, more lossy, optimizations can be applied to further decrease file size and increase execution speed, but due to this, the accuracy suffers a little.

To convert TF models into TFLite models, the TFLite converter is used, which is available as a Python API. In TF2.0, SavedModel directories, tf.keras models, and concrete functions can all be converted into TFLite format. A difference to note between TF1.x and TF2.0 is that frozen GraphDefs conversion is no longer supported in TF2.0, as is the case with models taken from the deprecated tf.Session model. If you need to save a frozen GraphDef in TFLite, tf.compat.v1.TFLiteConverter can be used. Only supported TF operations can be converted into TFLite format, and operations such as tf.depth_to_space, tf.image.resize_bilinear, and tf.tanh are not supported as of now. The following diagram illustrates the architecture of a TFLite model:

The following is an example of converting a SavedModel API into TFLite format:

1. Import the tensorflow library:

```
import tensorflow as tf
```

2. Construct a basic model:

```
root = tf.train.Checkpoint()
root.v1 = tf.Variable(3.)
root.v2 = tf.Variable(2.)
root.f = tf.function(lambda x: root.v1 * root.v2 * x)
```

3. Save the model:

```
export_dir = "/tmp/test_saved_model"
input_data = tf.constant(1., shape=[1, 1])
to_save = root.f.get_concrete_function(input_data)
tf.saved_model.save(root, export_dir, to_save)
```

4. Convert the model:

```
converter = tf.lite.TFLiteConverter.from_saved_model(export_dir)
tflite_model = converter.convert()
```

The following is an example of converting a tf.keras model into TFLite format:

1. Import the tensorflow library:

```
import tensorflow as tf
```

2. Create a simple Keras model:

```
x = [-1, 0, 1, 2, 3, 4]
y = [-3, -1, 1, 3, 5, 7]

model = tf.keras.models.Sequential(
    [tf.keras.layers.Dense(units=1, input_shape=[1])])
model.compile(optimizer='sgd', loss='mean_squared_error')
model.fit(x, y, epochs=50)
```

3. Convert the model:

```
converter = tf.lite.TFLiteConverter.from_keras_model(model)
tflite_model = converter.convert()
```

The following is an example of converting a function into TFLite format:

1. Import the `tensorflow` library:

```
import tensorflow as tf
```

2. Construct a basic model:

```
root = tf.train.Checkpoint()
root.v1 = tf.Variable(3.)
root.v2 = tf.Variable(2.)
root.f = tf.function(lambda x: root.v1 * root.v2 * x)
```

3. Create a `concrete` function:

```
input_data = tf.constant(1., shape=[1, 1])
concrete_func = root.f.get_concrete_function(input_data)

converter =
tf.lite.TFLiteConverter.from_concrete_functions([concrete_func])
tflite_model = converter.convert()
```

The next step, once the TF model has been converted, is to run inferences with the model. This utilizes the TFLite interpreter, which takes the model file, executes the operations defined on input data, and provides access to the output. The interpreter runs on many platforms, such as Java, Swift, Objective-C, C++, and Python.

Finally, the TFLite model can be optimized with an often minimal impact on accuracy. Some features TF provides are the model optimization toolkit and model quantization, which reduces the precision of values and operations within a model, thus reducing the size and the latency.

Running TFLite on mobile devices

In this section, we will cover how TFLite can be run on the two major mobile OSes: Android and iOS.

TFLite on Android

Using TFLite on Android is as easy as adding TFLite to the `dependencies` field in the `build.gradle` file in Android Studio, and importing it into Android Studio:

```
dependencies {
    implementation 'org.tensorflow:tensorflow-lite:0.0.0-nightly'
}

import org.tensorflow.lite.Interpreter;
```

Once this is done, the next step is to create an instance of the interpreter and load the model. This can be done using a `helper` function from the TFLite sample on GitHub called `getModelPath`, and by using `loadModelFile` to load the converted TFLite file. Now, to run the model, simply use the `.run` method of the interpreter class and give it the required input data, like in this example:

```
tflite.run(inp,out);
```

The `inp` argument is the input data that will be fed to the model, while `out` is a pre-initialized variable that will be populated with the output data from the model. This output can then be manipulated in order for it to be shown in the app.

TFLite on iOS

Using TFLite on iOS is a similar process, which includes installing the TFLite interpreter, loading the model, and running it. Once again, follow the steps in the *Getting started with TFLite* section in order to create and convert a machine learning model for use on a smartphone. We will use the following steps to implement TFLite on iOS:

1. Install TFLite by adding it to the `pod` file in the `root` directory of the project:

```
use_frameworks!
pod 'TensorFlowLiteSwift'
```

Install the package by running `pod install`, which will install all the packages included in the `pod` file, including the newly added `TFLite` package. Once installed, the package can be imported by adding `import TensorFlowLite` near the top of the `swift` file.

2. To run `interpreter`, first allocate the memory for the tensors:

```
let outputTensor: Tensor
do {
    try interpreter.allocateTensors()
    let inputTensor = try interpreter.input(at: 0)
```

3. Then, remove the `alpha` component from the image buffer to get the `rgbData` variable:

```
guard let rgbData = rgbDataFromBuffer(
thumbnailPixelBuffer,
byteCount: batchSize * inputWidth * inputHeight * inputChannels,
isModelQuantized: inputTensor.dataType == .uInt8
) else {
print("Failed to convert the image buffer to RGB data.")
return
}
```

4. Next, copy the `rgbData` variable to the `Tensor` input model:

```
try interpreter.copy(rgbData, toInputAt: 0)
```

5. Run inference by invoking the `interpreter` function:

```
try interpreter.invoke()
```

6. Get the `outputTensor` function to process the inference results:

```
outputTensor = try interpreter.output(at: 0)
} catch let error {
    print("Failed to invoke the interpreter with error:
\(error.localizedDescription)")
    return
}
```

The results can then be processed and displayed in the app.

Running TFLite on low-power machines

TFLite's capability of being able to run on low-power and low-binary machines makes it very powerful when run on embedded Linux machines. TFLite can be run on many of the popular embedded Linux machines, and as well as on the Coral Dev Board. In this section, we will cover the building, compiling, and running of TFLite on three devices. The first device that's covered is the Coral Dev Board with the Edge TPU processor, the second device is the NVIDIA Jetson Nano, and the final one is the Raspberry Pi. The NVIDIA Jetson Nano is a small and powerful computer from NVIDIA that runs multiple neural networks in parallel in applications such as image classification, object detection, segmentation, and speech processing.

Running TFLite on an Edge TPU processor

The Edge TPU is a small processor that is capable of executing deep feedforward networks, such as convolutional neural networks. However, it only supports quantized TFLite models. **Quantization** is an optimization technique that converts all of the 32-bit floating-point numbers into the nearest 8-bit fixed-point numbers. This makes the model smaller and faster, albeit a bit less precise and accurate.

Two types of quantization are supported in TF. The first style of quantization is **post-training quantization**. This is done at the time of conversion of the TF model into a TFLite model by setting the model optimization attribute to a list with `tf.lite.Optimize.OPTIMIZE_FOR_SIZE`. This causes the weights to be converted into 8-bit precision to increase latency by up to 3x. Other more compute-intensive operations in a network are converted into hybrid operations with fixed-point operations, but with floating-point memory.

The other type of quantization is **quantization-aware training**, which uses fake quantization nodes to simulate the effect of quantization in the forward-pass and the backward-pass models; this quantization is a straight-through estimation. This is the only quantization that is supported by the Edge TPU and allows the TFLite model to be run on it.

The Edge TPU is available in two ways:

- The Coral Dev Board, which contains the TPU and all required software and APIs preinstalled
- The Edge TPU USB extender, which adds another processor to the desired machine

The USB accelerator is compatible with any Linux computer with a USB port running Debian. To set up the USB accelerator, download the `.tar` file from `https://dl.google.com/coral/edgetpu_api/edgetpu_api_latest.tar.gz -O` `edgetpu_api.tar.gz--trust-server-names/`, then untar it and run `install.sh`.

 Something to note here is that, during the installation, the setup will ask to enable maximum operating frequency, which will speed up inference time significantly but also make the TPU very hot to touch.

The following diagram shows the process through which a TF model can be converted into an Edge TPU model and run on it:

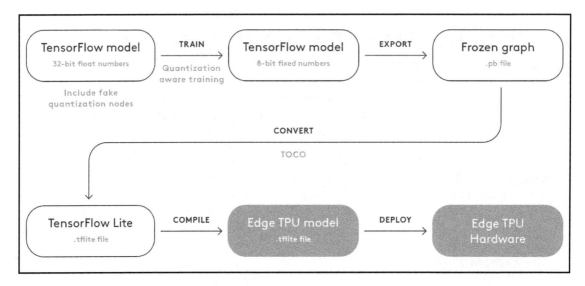

However, the Edge TPU has a couple of constraints. As we mentioned previously, the `Tensor` parameters must be quantized using quantize-aware training; the tensor sizes must be constant (so there can be no dynamic sizes); the model parameters must be constant; and tensors must either be one-, two-, or three-dimensional tensors or tensors whose three innermost dimensions are more than three, and must only contain those operations supported by the Edge TPU. If these requirements are not met, then only some of the models will compile. The first point in the model graph, where an unsupported operation occurs, is where the compiler splits the graph into two: one part containing all the operations the Edge TPU can compute, and the other part containing the operations it cannot compute, which are run on the CPU:

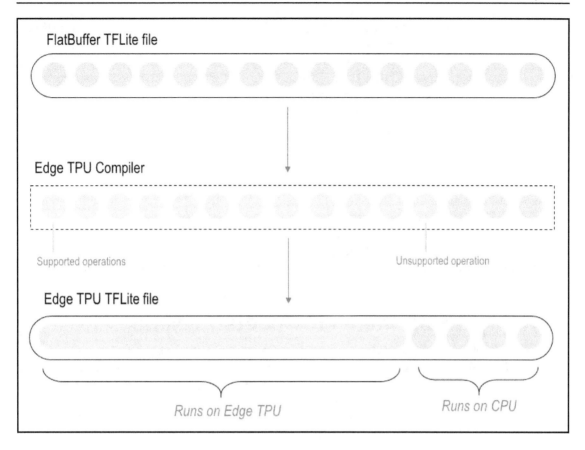

Once the TFLite model has been compiled and ready to run, it can be executed using the Edge TPU runtime and API library. The Edge TPU API has three key APIs for inferencing:

- The `ClassificationEngine` API, which performs image classification. To use it, create an instance by specifying a model, then pass an image to the instance's `ClassifyWithImage()` method, which returns a list of labels and scores.

- The `DetectionEngine` API, which performs object detection. Like the previous API, create an instance by specifying a model file, and then run the `DetectWithImage()` method, which returns a list of detection candidate objects, each of which contains a label, a score, and the coordinates of the object.

- The final key API is one that allows for imprinting: a transfer learning algorithm that allows for model retraining without backpropagation and can run on the Edge TPU. To run this API, three steps must be followed:
    1. First, identify the embedding tensor, which is the input tensor to the last classification layer.
    2. Then, cut off the last classification layer.
    3. Finally, complete the embedding extractor.

The performance of the Edge TPU is far superior to many of the most powerful CPUs. An individual Edge TPU is capable of performing 4 trillion operations per second using a total of 2 watts, when models were tested on an Intel Xeon(R) 3.60 GHz processor with and without the USB accelerator; an embedded 1.5 GHz CPU; and the Coral Dev Board. When running the DeepLab network, the Intel Xeon took 301 ms, the Intel Xeon with the accelerator took 35 ms, the embedded CPU took 1,210 ms, and the Coral Dev Board took 156 ms. It is clear that the Edge TPU has a major impact on the latency of the model.

Running TF on the NVIDIA Jetson Nano

The NVIDIA Jetson Nano is another embedded device that provides powerful computing power for machine learning applications. The premise of the Jetson Nano is different from the Edge TPU in the sense that the Jetson Nano is a small yet powerful GPU computer. The Jetson Nano can be used like any machine configured for deep learning, and the GPU version of TF can be installed simply enough. The installation of CUDA and cuDNN is also not needed as it is preinstalled on the system.

Comparing TFLite and TF

As we mentioned previously, TFLite models are quite different from the normal TF models. TFLite models are much faster, smaller in size, and less computationally expensive. This distinction comes from the special way TFLite models are stored and interpreted.

The first speed increase comes from the fundamental format the model is stored in. The `.tflite` model file is stored in a `FlatBuffer` format, containing a reduced and binary representation of the model. `FlatBuffer` is an efficient cross-platform serialization library for many popular languages and was created by Google for game development and other performance-critical applications. The `FlatBuffer` format plays an essential role in effectively serializing model data and providing quick access to that data while maintaining a small binary size. This is useful for model storage due to the huge amount of numerical data, which typically creates a lot of latency in read operations. By using `FlatBuffers`, TFLite can bypass many traditional file parsing and unparsing operations, which is very computationally expensive.

TFLite model optimizations also stretch all the way to the hardware on the device. This is because, due to the limitations of phone processors and embedded CPUs, all processors must be utilized at a hyper-efficient standard. When running TFLite on Android, the Android Neural Network API, which provides access to hardware-accelerated inference operations in Android, is interfaced to leverage advantageous hardware acceleration to the device being used. TFLite can also use the built-in GPUs in phones and other devices so that models with excess parallelizable operations and quantization-sensitive accuracy can be sped up by nearly 7x.

As we explained previously, quantization is another very impactful optimization technique. Quantization is viewed as a compression technique in TF. The weights and activations in neural networks tend to have three values that are distributed across relatively small ranges, so quantization can be used in great effect to compress the values. Since neural networks tend to be robust to noise in their weights, the noise that quantization and rounding add to the parameters has a minimal effect on the overall accuracy of the model. The benefits of a quantized model are that it efficiently represents an arbitrary magnitude of ranges, their linear spread makes multiplications straightforward, and the quantized weights have a symmetric range that enables downstream hardware optimizations that aren't possible with 32-bit floating point numbers.

As seen in the following graph, converting a model from TF into a quantized TFLite model greatly decreases the inference time and latency of a model:

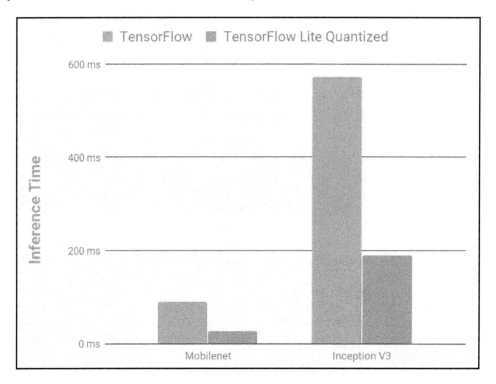

AIY

Google released their own maker kits for both voice and vision applications called AIY. These kits come shipped with all the required parts and components, along with easy-to-understand tutorials online. There are two kits currently offered by AIY—the Voice Kit and the Vision Kit.

The Voice Kit

The Voice Kit provides the functionality to build a natural language processor and connect it to the Google Assistant or the Cloud Speech-to-Text service. This kit comes shipped with a Raspberry Pi Zero, along with a custom-designed Voice Bonnet and a speaker for the audio capabilities. The kit also comes with an SD card that can be inserted into the Pi, and a multitude of demos, samples, and snippets for many of the most common applications. It also comes with an application that runs Google Assistant on the device and turns it into a smart home device.

To get started with the Voice Kit, follow the instructions to build the device at `https://aiyprojects.withgoogle.com/voice/#assembly-guide`. The device is well designed and is easy to assemble and set up. To set up the device, either a computer or a mobile phone can be used. The setup of the kit is simple and can be done through **Secure Shell** (**SSH**) or an HDMI connection. Once completed, there are many demos that can be run to further understand and explore the kit, such as the aforementioned Google Assistant application.

 Some things that can be done with the Voice Kit include creating a custom voice user interface and controlling an IoT device using the Assistant.

Creating a custom voice user interface on the Voice Kit can be done by using the Google Cloud Speech-to-Text API and the AIY APIs included in the `demo` folder of the kit. This API adds functionality for using the Cloud Speech API, Speech-to-Text, and for controlling the GPIO pins on the Vision Bonnet.

To control an IoT device using the Voice Kit and the Assistant, you can use a couple of powerful technologies. The Particle Photon, a Wi-Fi development kit for IoT projects, and `DialogFlow`, used to create the conversational interface, are both used. The demo included in the Voice Kit provides the code to turn an LED connected to the Photon on and off.

The Vision Kit

The Vision Kit provides the functionality to build an intelligent camera that can see and recognize objects using machine learning, and even run a custom TF model on it. Like the Voice Kit, this kit ships with a Raspberry Pi Zero, along with a custom-designed Vision Bonnet, a piezo buzzer, and the Raspberry Pi Camera V2. This kit comes with an SD card that is pre-flashed with the AIY system image, which includes demos for many kinds of computer vision applications such as image classification, object detection, face detection, food classification, and automatic photo-taking.

As before, the Vision Kit can be assembled by following the directions at `https://aiyprojects.withgoogle.com/vision/#assembly-guide`. The device has a simple and intuitive assembly that directs the user to neatly nestle the hardware and thread the wires, leading to a cool and sleek look. To set up the device, either a computer or a mobile phone can be used, and connecting to the device through SSH is also simple once the device is connected to the internet.

This kit also is capable of simply taking photos using the camera connected to the Pi. To do this, run the `raspistill -w width -h height -o image.jpg` command, where `width` and `height` are replaced by the desired dimensions of the photo in pixels. `raspistill` is a command that allows a user to capture photos using the Raspberry Pi camera module.

As we mentioned previously, there are many demos that can be tried on the Vision Kit. The first demo that runs by default on the kit is the Joy Detector. This uses a TFLite model to detect whether a person is smiling or frowning, and turns the button yellow if a smile is detected, or blue if a frown is detected. A sound is also played if the expression is really big and lots of joy is detected. You can also take a photo with the Joy Detector running, which will both take the desired picture and save an annotated copy of the joy scores of all the faces in the photo.

Other demos that run in real time include the image classification and face detection demos. Each demo can be started and will be run constantly. The demos log the model output to the shell when pertinent, along with the probabilities associated with each reading. To stop these demos, press *Ctrl + C* to return the prompt back to bash.

Another interesting demo provided with the Vision Kit is the ability to take a photo when a face is detected.

Demos such as object detection, face detection, and food classification require a photo to have been taken. These demos output more details on the model output, such as the bounding boxes for the detection demo and multiple predictions for the classification demo. Something to note here is that these demos run slower than the others since the model sizes are bigger and more complex.

The Vision Kit also allows the user to train custom models as well. However, only TFLite models are supported on the Vision Kit due to the limitations of the Raspberry Pi Zero. To convert a TF model into a TFLite model, refer to the *Getting started with TFLite* section. Along with the limitations that come with a TFLite model, there are a couple more limitations with the Vision Kit. These limitations are that the model must take a square RGB image and the input image size must be a multiple of 8, the model graph must be acyclic, the model must begin with `tf.nn.conv2d`, and the model should be trained with images in NHWC format.

Summary

TFLite is a feature of TF2.0 that takes a TF model and compresses and optimizes it to run on an embedded Linux device, or a low-power and low-binary device. Converting a TF model into a TFLite model can be done in three ways: from a saved model, a `tf.keras` model, or a concrete function. Once the model has been converted, a `.tflite` file will be created, which can then be transferred to the desired device and run using the TFLite interpreter. This model is optimized to use hardware acceleration and is stored in `FlatBuffer` format for quick read speeds. Other optimization techniques can be applied to the model, such as quantization, which converts the 32-bit floating point numbers into 8-bit fixed-point numbers, with a tradeoff of a minimal amount of accuracy. Some devices that TFLite can be run on are the Edge TPU, the NVIDIA Jetson Nano, and the Raspberry Pi. Google also provides two kits that start users with the hardware needed to create vision- and voice-related machine learning applications.

In the next chapter, we will learn how to migrate from TF1.x to TF2.0.

Section 4: TensorFlow 2.0 - Migration, Summary

This section of the book will summarize the use of **TensorFlow 2.0** (**TF 2.0**) in a high-level approach, as well as the compatibility differences of TF 2.0 compared with previous versions. This part of the book will focus on how to migrate to TF 2.0 if you have used **TensorFlow 1.x** (**TF 1.x**). Though there is a migration API to convert TF 1.x code to TF 2.0, it just does a syntax-to-syntax translation. This part will also dive deeper into guiding you through the code-level changes needed to convert TF 1.x code to TF 2.0 semantically.

This section contains the following chapter:

- Chapter 7, *Migrating From TensorFlow 1.x to 2.0*

Migrating From TensorFlow 1.x to 2.0

7

This chapter will cover how you can convert **TensorFlow 1.x (TF 1.x)** code into **TensorFlow 2.0 (TF 2.0)** code in two ways. The first method is to use the update script, which changes most of the TF 1.x code so that it can run in TF 2.0. This, however, simply converts all `tf.x` API calls into `tf.compat.v1.x` format. The other method is to convert TF 1.x code into idiomatic TF2.0 code by taking into account the core changes that have been made to the library. We will discuss the conceptual differences between TF 1.x and TF 2.0, the compatibility criteria between them, and the ways we can migrate syntactically and semantically. We will also show several examples of syntactic and semantic migration from TF 1.x to TF 2.0, with which we will provide references and future information.

The following topics will be covered in this chapter:

- Major changes in TF 2.0
- Recommended techniques to employ for idiomatic TF 2.0
- Making code TF 2.0 native
- Frequently asked questions
- The future of TF 2.0

Major changes in TF 2.0

The major changes that you will experience while migrating from TF 1.x to TF 2.0 concern API cleanup.

Many of the APIs in TF 2.0 have either been removed or moved. Major changes include the removal of `tf.app`, `tf.flags`, and `tf.logging` in favor of other Python modules, such as `absl-py` and the built-in logging system.

One of the largest changes that has been made in TF 2.0 code-wise is eager execution. TF 1.x requires users to manually stitch an abstract syntax tree using `tf.*` calls to build a computational graph, which it will run with `session.run()`. This means that TF 2.0 code runs line by line, and so `tf.control_dependancies()` is no longer needed.

The `session.run()` call in TF 1.x is very similar to a simple function. The user specifies the inputs and the function to be called, and it returns a set of outputs. This code flow is completely revamped in TF 2.0 through eager execution and function annotations such as `tf.function`.

As we mentioned previously in this book, using `tf.function` to annotate a function runs it in graph mode, which provides benefits such as performance and portability.

The final major change in TF 2.0 is that there are no more global variables. In TF 1.x, variables that were created using `tf.Variable` would be put on the default graph and would still be recoverable through its name. TF 1.x had all sorts of mechanisms in an effort to help users recover their variables, such as variable scopes, global collections, and helper methods, including `tf.get_global_step` and `tf.global_variables_initializer`. All of these have been removed in TF 2.0 in favor of the default variable behavior in Python.

Recommended techniques to employ for idiomatic TF 2.0

The first recommendation concerns dealing with a general code workflow in TF 2.0. A common workflow in TF 1.x was to use a waterfall strategy, where all of the computations were laid out onto the default graph. Then, selected tensors were run using `session.run()`. In TF 2.0, code should be refactored into smaller functions that will be called as needed. These functions can be normal Python functions and can still be run in graph mode if they're called inside another function annotated with `tf.function`. This means that `tf.function` should only be used to annotate high-level computations, such as the forward pass of a model or a single training step.

Previously, all of the computations that were needed for the model and training loop would be predetermined and written, and were executed using `session.run()`. This made TF 1.x code difficult to follow for most coders as the flow of the model could be significantly different from the way it was coded, as the graph was run at the very end. Eager execution and `tf.function` were created specifically to simplify TensorFlow code dynamics and make it easier for other developers to understand prewritten code.

Managing and keeping track of variables was another complicated process in TF 1.x. Many methods were used to control and access these variables, which added even more dimensions to what should be linear code. TF 2.0 places more emphasis on using `tf.keras` layers and `tf.estimator` models to manage the variables in a model.

This is a contrast from hand-rolling neural network layers and creating the variables manually. In the following example, the weight and bias variables have to be kept track of, with their shapes defined away from the model's creation. This makes it difficult to change and adapt the model to different architectures and datasets:

```
def dense(x, W, b):
  return tf.nn.sigmoid(tf.matmul(x, W) + b)

@tf.function
def multilayer_perceptron(x, w0, b0, w1, b1, w2, b2 ...):
    x = dense(x, w0, b0)
    x = dense(x, w1, b1)
    x = dense(x, w2, b2)
    ...
```

The `tf.keras` implementation of this code is straightforward, concise, and ensures that the developer doesn't worry about the organization and management of variables and variable names. It provides easy access to the trainable variables in the model as well:

```
layers = [tf.keras.layers.Dense(hidden_size, activation=tf.nn.sigmoid) for
_ in range(n)]
perceptron = tf.keras.Sequential(layers)

# layers[3].trainable_variables => returns [w3, b3]
# perceptron.trainable_variables => returns [w0, b0, ...]
```

`tf.keras` models also inherit methods from the `tf.train.Checkpointable` model and are integrated with `tf.function` so that they can be directly saved to a checkpoint and exported to `SavedModels`.

The following is an example of a transfer learning implementation, and shows how `tf.keras` makes it easy to collect a subset of relevant values, calculate their gradients, and tune them based on the gradients:

```
trunk = tf.keras.Sequential([...])
head1 = tf.keras.Sequential([...])
head2 = tf.keras.Sequential([...])

path1 = tf.keras.Sequential([trunk, head1])
path2 = tf.keras.Sequential([trunk, head2])
```

```
# Train on primary dataset
for x, y in main_dataset:
  with tf.GradientTape() as tape:
    prediction = path1(x)
    loss = loss_fn_head1(prediction, y)
  # Simultaneously optimize trunk and head1 weights.
  gradients = tape.gradient(loss, path1.trainable_variables)
  optimizer.apply_gradients(zip(gradients, path1.trainable_variables))

# Fine-tune second head, reusing the trunk
for x, y in small_dataset:
  with tf.GradientTape() as tape:
    prediction = path2(x)
    loss = loss_fn_head2(prediction, y)
  # Only optimize head2 weights, not trunk weights
  gradients = tape.gradient(loss, head2.trainable_variables)
  optimizer.apply_gradients(zip(gradients, head2.trainable_variables))

# You can publish just the trunk computation for other people to reuse.
tf.saved_model.save(trunk, output_path)
```

All of the datasets that aren't already stored in memory should be stored and streamed using `tf.dataset`. Datasets are iterables in TF 2.0, and so they can be used like any other Python iterable, such as lists and tuples, in eager execution mode. You can also take advantage of dataset async prefetching and streaming features by wrapping a dataset iteration with `tf.function`, which converts a Python interaction into the equivalent graph operations with AutoGraph. As we mentioned earlier in the book, AutoGraph takes the default Python flow and converts it into graph-based code. For example, control flows such as `if...else` blocks are converted into `tf.condition` statements. The following code block shows you how to train a model with a `for` block:

```
@tf.function
def train(model, dataset, optimizer):
  for x, y in dataset:
    with tf.GradientTape() as tape:
      prediction = model(x)
      loss = loss_fn(prediction, y)
    gradients = tape.gradient(loss, model.trainable_variables)
    optimizer.apply_gradients(zip(gradients, model.trainable_variables))
```

However, if you're using Keras' `model.fit`, then this isn't something to be worried about. To train a model on a dataset using `model.fit`, simply pass the dataset to the method. It will take care of everything else:

```
model.compile(optimizer=optimizer, loss=loss_fn)
model.fit(dataset)
```

Making code TF 2.0-native

The simplest way to make TF 1.x code compatible with TF 2.0 code is to run the update script that's installed on your system, along with the TF 2.0 installation. The update script makes use of the `tf.compat.v1` module.

As a way to provide backward compatibility for code written for TF 1.x, the `tf.compat.v1` module was introduced in TF 2.0. The `tf.compat.v1` module replaces all TF 1.x symbols, such as `tf.foo` and `tf.compat.v1.foo`. This module allows most of the code that's been written for TF 1.x to be converted so that it can be run in TF 2.0.

As a way to streamline this process, TensorFlow provides a `tf_upgrade_v2` utility, which helps streamline the transition as much as possible. This utility is preinstalled with the TF 2.0 installation, along with any TF 1.x installation from r1.13 and onwards. To run this script, simply specify an `infile` and `outfile` variable. This will run it on a single Python file:

```
tf_upgrade_v2 --infile tensorfoo.py --outfile tensorfoo-upgraded.py
```

Alternatively, use the following script to modify the entire directory and create a new directory with all the files that have been either copied over or converted from TF 1.x into TF 2.0 format:

```
tf_upgrade_v2 --intree coolcode --outtree coolcode-upgraded
```

This script also provides a detailed report of the changes that have been made, and the issues that could not be changed by the script and that need manual attention.

Some caveats to this script are that the modules that have been deprecated in TF 2.0, such as `tf.flags` and `tf.contrib`, cannot be converted from TF 1.x into TF 2.0 and will need additional modules to be installed or require the user to switch to a package from TensorFlow or Addons.

The script also won't reorder arguments in functions, and will only add keyword arguments to functions with arguments that have been reordered in TF 2.0. For the script to function, `tensorflow` must be imported as `tf`, as follows:

```
import tensorflow as tf
```

The downsides of using this update script is that the flow of the code won't change, and the code does not benefit from the improvements that were made in TF 2.0. To make TensorFlow code into v2.0, there are four major steps to follow. Let's go over this now.

Converting TF 1.x models

The first step is to replace all `tf.Session.run()` calls with a Python function. This means turning `tf.placeholder` and `feed_dict` into function arguments. These become the function's return value. This change means that standard Python tools such as `pdb` can be used to step through and debug the function, unlike TF 1.x. Once the function has been built, the `tf.function` annotation can be added to run the function in graph mode, along with the efficiency of the equivalent `tf.Session.run` calls in TF 1.x.

TF 1.x models that are created using the `tf.layers` API can be converted into TF 2.0 with relative ease. The `tf.layers` module was used to contain layer functions that relied on `tf.variable_scope` to define and reuse variables.

The following code block is an implementation of a small convolutional neural network in TF 1.x that's been written using the `tf.layers` API:

```
def model(x, training, scope='model'):
  with tf.variable_scope(scope, reuse=tf.AUTO_REUSE):
    x = tf.layers.conv2d(x, 32, 3, activation=tf.nn.relu,
        kernel_regularizer=tf.contrib.layers.l2_regularizer(0.04))
    x = tf.layers.max_pooling2d(x, (2, 2), 1)
    x = tf.layers.flatten(x)
    x = tf.layers.dropout(x, 0.1, training=training)
    x = tf.layers.dense(x, 64, activation=tf.nn.relu)
    x = tf.layers.batch_normalization(x, training=training)
    x = tf.layers.dense(x, 10, activation=tf.nn.softmax)
    return x

train_out = model(train_data, training=True)
test_out = model(test_data, training=False)
```

The simplest way to convert this model into TF 2.0 is by using `tf.keras.Sequential` since this model is made up of linear layers. There is a one-to-one conversion from `tf.layers` to `tf.keras.layers`, with a couple of differences. In TF 2.0 code, the training argument is no longer passed to each layer as the model handles that automatically.

Here is the code in TF 2.0:

```
model = tf.keras.Sequential([
    tf.keras.layers.Conv2D(32, 3, activation='relu',
kernel_regularizer=tf.keras.regularizers.l2(0.04),
                           input_shape=(28, 28, 1)),
    tf.keras.layers.MaxPooling2D(),
    tf.keras.layers.Flatten(),
    tf.keras.layers.Dropout(0.1),
    tf.keras.layers.Dense(64, activation='relu'),
    tf.keras.layers.BatchNormalization(),
    tf.keras.layers.Dense(10, activation='softmax')
])

train_data = tf.ones(shape=(1, 28, 28, 1))
test_data = tf.ones(shape=(1, 28, 28, 1))

train_out = model(train_data)

test_out = model(test_data, training=False)
```

As we can see, `tf.variable_scope` isn't used to organize the variables that were created for the model. In TF 1.x, this scope would be used to recover the variables from the model. In TF 2.0, the model variables can be listed using `model.trainable_variables`.

Although converting from `tf.layers` to `tf.keras.layers` is relatively simple, the conversion becomes more involved due to differences in code flow.

Some examples of low-level APIs in TF 1.x include using variable scopes to control reuse, creating variables using `tf.get_variable`, accessing collections regularly, using `tf.placeholder` and `session.run`, and initializing variables manually. Many of these techniques and strategies are now obsolete due to the introduction of system-wide eager execution, so code written in low-level APIs need a larger change than those written in high-level APIs, such as `tf.keras` and `tf.layers`.

The following is an example of some code that was written in the low-level APIs of TF 1.x:

```
in_a = tf.placeholder(dtype=tf.float32, shape=(2))
in_b = tf.placeholder(dtype=tf.float32, shape=(2))

def forward(x):
  with tf.variable_scope("matmul", reuse=tf.AUTO_REUSE):
    W = tf.get_variable("W", initializer=tf.ones(shape=(2,2)),
                        regularizer=tf.contrib.layers.l2_regularizer(0.04))
    b = tf.get_variable("b", initializer=tf.zeros(shape=(2)))
    return W * x + b
```

```
out_a = forward(in_a)
out_b = forward(in_b)

reg_loss = tf.losses.get_regularization_loss(scope="matmul")

with tf.Session() as sess:
  sess.run(tf.global_variables_initializer())
  outs = sess.run([out_a, out_b, reg_loss],
                  feed_dict={in_a: [1, 0], in_b: [0, 1]})
```

This code can be converted by changing the forward function to a function annotated with tf.function for graph-based computation, and removing the session.run function and variable scope and adding a simple function call. The regularization will not be called globally on the W variable; instead, it will be called manually, without needing to refer to a global collection:

```
W = tf.Variable(tf.ones(shape=(2,2)), name="W")
b = tf.Variable(tf.zeros(shape=(2)), name="b")

@tf.function
def forward(x):
  return W * x + b

out_a = forward([1,0])
out_b = forward([0,1])

regularizer = tf.keras.regularizers.l2(0.04)
reg_loss = regularizer(W)
```

As we can see, the TF 2.0 code is much more Pythonic and concise than the previous TF 1.x code.

One of the benefits of using tf.placeholder was that the shape of the input of the graph could be controlled and would return an error if it did not match the predetermined shape. This can still be done in TF 2.0 through the use of the assert command that's built into Python. This can be used to assert that the shape of the input arguments to the function matches what is expected from the input arguments.

Existing TF 1.x code often includes both lower-level TF 1.x variables and operations with higher-level tf.layers. This means that neither of the preceding examples will be sufficient to convert the TF 1.x code, and requires a more complex form of tf.keras programming called model or layer subclassing.

The following is the original code that was written in TF 1.x that uses both
`tf.get_variable` and `tf.layers`:

```
def model(x, training, scope='model'):
  with tf.variable_scope(scope, reuse=tf.AUTO_REUSE):
    W = tf.get_variable(
        "W", dtype=tf.float32,
        initializer=tf.ones(shape=x.shape),
        regularizer=tf.contrib.layers.l2_regularizer(0.04),
        trainable=True)
    if training:
      x = x + W
    else:
      x = x + W * 0.5
    x = tf.layers.conv2d(x, 32, 3, activation=tf.nn.relu)
    x = tf.layers.max_pooling2d(x, (2, 2), 1)
    x = tf.layers.flatten(x)
    return x

train_out = model(train_data, training=True)
test_out = model(test_data, training=False)
```

This code can be converted by wrapping all of the low-level operations and variables inside
a custom created Keras layer. This can be done by creating a class that inherits from the
`tf.keras.layers.Layer` class:

```
# Create a custom layer for part of the model
class CustomLayer(tf.keras.layers.Layer):
  def __init__(self, *args, **kwargs):
    super(CustomLayer, self).__init__(*args, **kwargs)

  def build(self, input_shape):
    self.w = self.add_weight(
        shape=input_shape[1:],
        dtype=tf.float32,
        initializer=tf.keras.initializers.ones(),
        regularizer=tf.keras.regularizers.l2(0.02),
        trainable=True)

  # Call method will sometimes get used in graph mode,
  # training will get turned into a tensor
  @tf.function
  def call(self, inputs, training=None):
    if training:
      return inputs + self.w
    else:
      return inputs + self.w * 0.5
```

The preceding code creates a class called `CustomLayer`, which inherits attributes from the `tf.keras.layers.Layer` class. This is a technique that allows any sort of low-level code to be used inside of a `tf.keras` model, regardless of whether it is a model that uses the `Sequential` API or `functional` API. There are two methods inside this class:

- `build()`: This method modifies the default build method of the inherited class. In this method, all of the variables that are needed for the model should be created. Although this can be done inside the the `__init__()` method of the model, using `build()` is recommended so that the variables are built at the correct and most optimal time. This can be done using the `self.add_weight` function to allow Keras to keep track of the variables and regularization losses.
- `call()`: This method is run when the model is called on an input tensor. This method typically takes two arguments: `inputs` and `training`. While the `inputs` argument is self-explanatory, the `training` argument might not be used all the time, but is necessary for when batch normalization and dropout are used in the layer. This function is annotated with the `tf.function` decorator for autograph, graph-based benefits, and automatic control dependencies.

Once this custom layer has been written, it can be used anywhere in the `tf.keras` module. For this conversion, the `Sequential` API will be used:

```
train_data = tf.ones(shape=(1, 28, 28, 1))
test_data = tf.ones(shape=(1, 28, 28, 1))

# Build the model including the custom layer
model = tf.keras.Sequential([
    CustomLayer(input_shape=(28, 28, 1)),
    tf.keras.layers.Conv2D(32, 3, activation='relu'),
    tf.keras.layers.MaxPooling2D(),
    tf.keras.layers.Flatten(),
])

train_out = model(train_data, training=True)
test_out = model(test_data, training=False)
```

Upgrading training loops

The second step of converting TF 1.x code into idiomatic TF 2.0 code is to upgrade the training pipelines. TF 1.x training pipelines involve multiple `tf.Session.run()` calls for the optimizer, losses, and predictions. Such training loops also involve boilerplate code that's written to log the training results to the console for easy supervision.

In TF 2.0, three types of training loops can be used. Each of these loops has different advantages and disadvantages and varies in difficulty, API level, and complexity. They are as follows:

- The first type of training loop is `tf.keras.Model.fit()`. This is a built-in training loop that handles all the aspects of training and provides a uniform interface for all kinds of Keras models, whether they be `Sequential`, `Functional`, or `SubClassed`. This method goes along with `tf.keras.Model.evaluate()` and `tf.keras.Model.predict()`, which are very high-level methods that can perform in an efficient and uniform way. The advantages of using `tf.keras.Model.fit` include compatibility with Python iterables, NumPy arrays, and `tf.data.Datasets`; support for regularization and activation loss; the use of `tf.distribute` for multi-device training; and callbacks such as `tf.keras.callbacks.Tensorboard`.

  The following is an example of training a model using `tf.data.Dataset` and `tf.keras.Model.fit()`:

  ```
  model = tf.keras.Sequential([
      tf.keras.layers.Conv2D(32, 3, activation='relu',
  kernel_regularizer=tf.keras.regularizers.l2(0.02),
                          input_shape=(28, 28, 1)),
      tf.keras.layers.MaxPooling2D(),
      tf.keras.layers.Flatten(),
      tf.keras.layers.Dropout(0.1),
      tf.keras.layers.Dense(64, activation='relu'),
      tf.keras.layers.BatchNormalization(),
      tf.keras.layers.Dense(10, activation='softmax')
  ])

  # Model is the full model w/o custom layers
  model.compile(optimizer='adam',
                loss='sparse_categorical_crossentropy',
                metrics=['accuracy'])

  model.fit(train_data, epochs=NUM_EPOCHS)
  loss, acc = model.evaluate(test_data)

  print("Loss {}, Accuracy {}".format(loss, acc))
  ```

  As can be seen in the preceding example, the `tf.data.Dataset` object is simply passed to the `tf.keras.Model.fit()` function like any other Python iterator that's used for training the model.

- The second, more complex type of training loop in TF 2.0 is one that uses `tf.keras.Model.train_on_batch()`, a custom data iteration, and an outer loop. This method retains most of the advantages of the previous type, but provides control over the outer training loop to the user. This type of training is used when the user wants to implement a custom training loop, and can be used when you have to train two or more models that are dependent on each other.

The following is an example of training using `tf.keras.Model.train_on_batch()`:

```
model.compile(optimizer='adam',
              loss='sparse_categorical_crossentropy',
              metrics=['accuracy'])

metrics_names = model.metrics_names

for epoch in range(NUM_EPOCHS):
  #Reset the metric accumulators
  model.reset_metrics()

  for image_batch, label_batch in train_data:
    result = model.train_on_batch(image_batch, label_batch)
    print("train: ",
          "{}: {:.3f}".format(metrics_names[0], result[0]),
          "{}: {:.3f}".format(metrics_names[1], result[1]))
  for image_batch, label_batch in test_data:
    result = model.test_on_batch(image_batch, label_batch,
                                 # return accumulated metrics
                                 reset_metrics=False)
  print("\neval: ",
        "{}: {:.3f}".format(metrics_names[0], result[0]),
        "{}: {:.3f}".format(metrics_names[1], result[1]))
```

- The final type of training loop is the most complex and customizable in TF 2.0. This entails creating a completely new training loop using lower-level APIs, such as `tf.GradientTape`. The three steps of this process are detailed extensively in Chapter 4, *Model Training and the Use of TensorBoard*. Basically, we need to iterate over the Python generator or `tf.data.Dataset`, use `tf.GradientTape` to collect the gradients, and use the `tf.keras.optimizer` function to apply weight updates to the model's variables. Please note that the user must handle regularization and activation losses manually.

This approach to training a model is similar to the typical training pipeline in TF 1.x. In TF 1.x, the code would iterate through the dataset, run the optimizer to update the variables using `tf.Session.run()`, and compute the losses and predictions to calculate and accumulate the training metrics. There are two major differences between this style of training and the training in TF 1.x. The first difference is that there is no need to run a variable initializer, as variables are initialized automatically at the time of creation. The second major difference is that there is no need to add manual control dependencies since all code – even code in `tf.function` – acts in eager mode. This means that all the code runs line by line, in the default Python fashion.

The following code block is an implementation of the training loop using `tf.GradientTape`:

```
model = tf.keras.Sequential([
    tf.keras.layers.Conv2D(32, 3, activation='relu',
kernel_regularizer=tf.keras.regularizers.l2(0.02),
                            input_shape=(28, 28, 1)),
    tf.keras.layers.MaxPooling2D(),
    tf.keras.layers.Flatten(),
    tf.keras.layers.Dropout(0.1),
    tf.keras.layers.Dense(64, activation='relu'),
    tf.keras.layers.BatchNormalization(),
    tf.keras.layers.Dense(10, activation='softmax')
])

optimizer = tf.keras.optimizers.Adam(0.001)
loss_fn = tf.keras.losses.SparseCategoricalCrossentropy()

@tf.function
def train_step(inputs, labels):
  with tf.GradientTape() as tape:
    predictions = model(inputs, training=True)
    regularization_loss = tf.math.add_n(model.losses)
    pred_loss = loss_fn(labels, predictions)
    total_loss = pred_loss + regularization_loss

  gradients = tape.gradient(total_loss, model.trainable_variables)
  optimizer.apply_gradients(zip(gradients,
model.trainable_variables))

for epoch in range(NUM_EPOCHS):
  for inputs, labels in train_data:
    train_step(inputs, labels)
  print("Finished epoch", epoch)
```

Other things to note when converting

There are a couple of other major conversions that are required when migrating from TF 1.x to TF 2.0. A conversation that is significantly more difficult than the ones we previously described is converting code written in TF-Slim to TF 2.0.

Since TF-Slim was packaged under the `tf.contrib.layers` library, it is not available in TF 2.0, even in the compatibility module. This means that to convert TF-Slim code into TF 2.0 format, the entire code dynamic often needs to be changed.

This includes removing argument scopes from code, as all arguments should be explicit in TF 2.0. The `normalizer_fn` and `activation_fn` functions should be split into their own layers. Note that TF-Slim layers have different argument names and default values than `tf.keras` layers.

The easiest way to convert a TF-Slim model into TF 2.0 is to convert it into the `tf.layers` API in TF 1.x, and then convert that into `tf.keras.layers`.

Another conversion detail to note is that, in TF 2.0, all metrics are objects that have three main methods: `update_state()`, which adds new observations, `result()`, which gets the current result of the metric, and `reset_states()`, which clears all observations.

Metrics objects are also callable, and when called on new observations, they accumulate the values and return the latest result.

The following example shows us how to use metrics in a custom training loop:

1. Create the metric objects that accumulate the metric data every time they are called:

```
loss_metric = tf.keras.metrics.Mean(name='train_loss')
accuracy_metric =
tf.keras.metrics.SparseCategoricalAccuracy(name='train_accuracy')

@tf.function
def train_step(inputs, labels):
  with tf.GradientTape() as tape:
    predictions = model(inputs, training=True)
    regularization_loss = tf.math.add_n(model.losses)
    pred_loss = loss_fn(labels, predictions)
    total_loss = pred_loss + regularization_loss

  gradients = tape.gradient(total_loss, model.trainable_variables)
  optimizer.apply_gradients(zip(gradients,
model.trainable_variables))
```

2. Update the metrics:

```
loss_metric.update_state(total_loss)
  accuracy_metric.update_state(labels, predictions)


for epoch in range(NUM_EPOCHS):
```

3. Reset the metrics:

```
loss_metric.reset_states()
  accuracy_metric.reset_states()

  for inputs, labels in train_data:
    train_step(inputs, labels)
```

4. Get the metric results:

```
mean_loss = loss_metric.result()
mean_accuracy = accuracy_metric.result()

print('Epoch: ', epoch)
print(' loss: {:.3f}'.format(mean_loss))
print(' accuracy: {:.3f}'.format(mean_accuracy))
```

Frequently asked questions

In this section, some frequently asked questions about the migration from TF 1.x to TF 2.0 will be addressed.

Does code written in TF 2.0 have the same speed as graph-based TF 1.x code?

Yes, code written in TF 2.0 using `tf.function` or `tf.keras` will have the same speed and optimality as it does in TF 1.x. As we mentioned earlier in this chapter, using `tf.function` to annotate major functions allows the model to be run in graph mode, and all the computations and logic in the function will be compiled into a computational graph. The same goes for using `tf.keras` to define and train TensorFlow models. Using the `model.fit` method will also train the model in graph mode and has all of the benefits and optimizations that come with this. When writing eager executed code, there is a slight performance drop, something which is more than compensated for by the other qualities of eager execution, such as straightforward code flow and easy debugging.

How do I control the input shape in TF 2.0, similar to setting the input shape for placeholders?

The analogy that was given in this chapter is to translate a tensor being computed using `sess.run` in TF 1.x code into a function in TF 2.0 code. The tensor itself becomes the function, `feed_dict` becomes the arguments of the function, and the `sess.run` call becomes a function call using the default Python syntax. In TF 1.x code, placeholders can be created that will have a fixed input shape, and feeding a tensor that doesn't match this shape would lead to an error. Although there is no native TensorFlow API in TF 2.0, the built-in Python `assert` command can be used in this situation. To do this, simply assert that the input arguments' shape matches a predetermined shape, and just like in TF 1.x code, if the input shape differs, an error will be raised. When writing `tf.keras` models with the `functional` API, the user can use the `tf.keras.layers.Input` class to define the input shape of the model, which is analogous to defining the placeholder at the beginning of the model in TF 1.x.

How does model checkpointing work in TF 2.0 if computations are not recorded on a graph?

Model checkpointing in TF 2.0 has been simplified greatly. If a model is defined using `tf.keras` APIs, a model checkpoint callback can simply be passed to the `model.fit` method, and all of the weights and metadata of the model will be saved. The callback can also be configured to customize how frequently the checkpoints should be saved in the training process. To restore weights using checkpoints in `tf.keras`, use the `model.load_weights` method and pass the checkpoint file to the method. `tf.keras` models can also be saved in HDF5 format. This saves the model into a single file which is self-contained and sufficient to load the entire model in `tf.keras`. To save models that have been created with low-level APIs, you can use the model subclassing method of defining TensorFlow models. This provides such models with all of the benefits and features of `tf.keras.Model` and allows for model checkpointing as well.

The future of TF 2.0

TF 2.0 is currently in beta and hence is still under development. Some key features that are coming up include modifications to packages such as TensorBoard, TensorFlow Lite, TensorFlow.js, Swift for TensorFlow, and TensorFlow Extended, and small changes being made to the base API. TensorBoard will see enhancements such as improved hyperparameter-tuning capabilities, the introduction of hosting capabilities to make sharing dashboards easy, and enabling plugins to use different frontend technologies, such as ReactJS. TensorFlow Lite will see increased coverage of supported operations, an easier conversion of TF 2.0 models to TFLite, and extended support for Edge TPUs and AIY boards. Both TensorFlow.js and Swift for TensorFlow will see improvements in speed and performance, and will soon include a rich set of examples and getting-started guides with end-to-end tutorials. TF Extended will soon have complete integration with the TF 2.0 base API and will include fully orchestrated end-to-end workflows and training features.

The TF 2.0 base API will include more premade estimators for tasks, such as boosted trees, random forests, nearest neighbor search, and k-means clustering. The `tf.distribute.Strategy` model will expand its support for Keras subclassed models, TPUs, and multi-node training for more optimized and faster training on multiple processors.

Another major addition that is currently being developed is the `tf-agents` module. This module implements the core reinforcement learning algorithms as **agents**, which define a policy for interacting with the environment and training the policy from a collective experience. `TF-agents` is implemented alongside the OpenAI Gym framework and abstracts many key reinforcement learning algorithms for use in development. This module is currently in its prerelease state, but it will be released later this year.

More resources to look at

Tutorials and many other resources can be found on the TensorFlow Beta website, which contains information on key factors in creating and training machine learning models. This page also has many useful end-to-end tutorials for many of the prominent technologies in the field (`https://www.tensorflow.org/beta`).

The official documentation for TF 2.0 can be found on the website, as well as detailed documentation on each of the APIs in the module. This site also has links to other TensorFlow modules and features (`https://www.tensorflow.org/versions/r2.0/api_docs/python/tf`).

The TensorFlow Medium blog also features many updates on the state of TensorFlow libraries and services and has a steady flow of useful news and tutorials on real-world applications of TF 2.0. The account also frequently posts useful tips and suggestions for novice and advanced users of TF 2.0, along with best practices (`https://medium.com/@tensorflow`).

Summary

This chapter covered two ways to convert TF 1.x code into TF 2.0 code. The first way is to use the included upgrade script, which changes all API calls from `tf.x` to `tf.compat.v1.x`. This allows TF 1.x code to run in TF 2.0, but will not benefit from the upgrades that were brought in TF 2.0. The second way is to change TF 1.x to idiomatic TF 2.0 code, which involves two steps. The first step is to change all model creation code into TF 2.0 code, which involves changing tensors using `sess.run` calls into functions, and placeholders and feed dicts into arguments for the function. Models that are created using the `tf.layers` API have a one-to-one comparison to `tf.keras.layers`. The second step is to upgrade the training pipeline by using either `tf.keras.Model.fit` or a custom training loop with `tf.GradientTape`.

TF 2.0 brings many changes in the way TensorFlow code is written and organized. Some major changes in TF 2.0 are the reorganization and cleanup of the APIs in the main module. This includes the removal of the `tf.contrib` module. Other changes include the addition of code-wide eager execution to allow for easier debugging and simpler usage. Because of eager execution, variables that are created in TF 2.0 will behave like normal Python variables. This means that TF 1.x APIs for handling global variables are obsolete and thus have been removed in TF 2.0. This brings us to the end of the book!

Other Books You May Enjoy

If you enjoyed this book, you may be interested in these other books by Packt:

TensorFlow 2.0 Quick Start Guide
Tony Holdroyd

ISBN: 9781789530759

- Use tf.Keras for fast prototyping, building, and training deep learning neural network models
- Easily convert your TensorFlow 1.12 applications to TensorFlow 2.0-compatible files
- Use TensorFlow to tackle traditional supervised and unsupervised machine learning applications
- Understand image recognition techniques using TensorFlow
- Perform neural style transfer for image hybridization using a neural network
- Code a recurrent neural network in TensorFlow to perform text-style generation

Hands-On Computer Vision with TensorFlow 2

Benjamin Planche and Eliot Andres

ISBN: 9781788830645

- Create your own neural networks from scratch
- Classify images with modern architectures including Inception and ResNet
- Detect and segment objects in images with YOLO, Mask R-CNN, and U-Net
- Tackle problems faced when developing self-driving cars and facial emotion recognition systems
- Boost your application's performance with transfer learning, GANs, and domain adaptation
- Use recurrent neural networks (RNNs) for video analysis
- Optimize and deploy your networks on mobile devices and in the browser

Leave a review - let other readers know what you think

Please share your thoughts on this book with others by leaving a review on the site that you bought it from. If you purchased the book from Amazon, please leave us an honest review on this book's Amazon page. This is vital so that other potential readers can see and use your unbiased opinion to make purchasing decisions, we can understand what our customers think about our products, and our authors can see your feedback on the title that they have worked with Packt to create. It will only take a few minutes of your time, but is valuable to other potential customers, our authors, and Packt. Thank you!

Index

CPSIA information can be obtained
at www.ICGtesting.com
Printed in the USA
LVHW101954140120
643594LV00010B/519